# BUILDING UNITED JUDGMENT

## A HANDBOOK FOR CONSENSUS DECISION MAKING

Michel Avery                    Brian Auvine

Barbara Streibel                Lonnie Weiss

A publication of:

The Fellowship for Intentional Community
Route 1, Box 155
Rutledge, MO 63563
1-800-995-8342

With invaluable assistance from Intra-Community Cooperative,
Elaine Nesterick, Education Coordinator


And significant contribution from Janice Kinsolving


Editorial assistance by Jan Stempel


Cover and graphics by Paulette Hurdlik

BUILDING UNITED JUDGMENT

A HANDBOOK FOR CONSENSUS DECISION MAKING

# Acknowledgements

We wish to thank Intra-Community Cooperative for their support and involvement in this writing project, especially as represented by the extensive contributions of Elaine Nesterick, Education Coordinator. We also wish to recognize Jan Stempel for her editorial help and consultation, which she provided both as an ICC representative and independently.

In addition, we want to acknowledge the active and enthusiastic participation of Janice Kinsolving which was a significant force in the development of this book.

We are grateful to Design Coalition for their advice and help in designing the format and for creating graphics, especially to Paulette Burdlik and Marlene (Beanie) Goodman for their contributions as representatives of Design Coalition and as individuals.

Bob Hopkins and Joe Folger participated in early planning and provided feedback on our work. Scott Poole wrote the first draft of the chapter which is now titled *WORKING WITH EMOTIONS*, and he provided comments on other chapters.

Our friend Crepps Wickliffe gave us extensive editorial feedback and helped write some sections. We regret that he is no longer alive to see the product of our efforts.

In addition, helpful comments on early drafts were offered by reviewers Jeff Haines, Trudy Cooper, Jim Crowfoot, Agnes Hole, Michael Ducey, Jim Struve, Betsy Densmore, Kirk Lawler, Ted Parker, Ailsa Steckel, Susan Jarboe, Cheryl Fraracci and Si Griffin. Many excellent ideas, criticisms and suggestions were given to us, not all of which are incorporated into this final version, simply because we could not do everything that deserved to be done.

We received advice about production and distribution from Dick McCleester, Peggy Butkereit and Bob Pfefferkorn.

We want to thank the Wisconsin Center for Public Policy for allowing us to use their offices for our final layout and paste-up. And we want to thank all the people who participated in that process--production logistics prevent us from including their names. Thanks too for the help of those whose names we have forgotten to mention. We're sure we've left out more than a few.

Finally, thanks to all our friends and associates, including, but not limited to, Marilyn Chapman, Roger Volkema, Lydia Larrabee, Celeste Rice, Sue Brummel, Marci Friedman and Curt Olson. We appreciate their patience, encouragement and support during the long stretches when it looked like we'd never finish.

## INTRODUCTION TO THIS PRINTING

In the past 25 years there has been an explosion of interest in consensus as a decision-making process that brings people together. Coming out of roots in the Religious Society of Friends (Quakers) and various Native American cultures, consensus got a fresh look among political activists in the 60's and 70's and much of that experience was concentrated in books which first appeared two decades ago. The magnum opus of the Philadelphia-based Movement for a New Society (MNS) was their 1976 guidebook to grassroots organizing, Manual for a Living Revolution.

At about the same time, the Center for Conflict Resolution (CCR) in Madison, Wisconsin, produced its pair of process classics, Building United Judgment (1981) and A Manual for Group Facilitators (1977), offering a blueprint for how to engage the whole person and the whole group. Today there are a handful of books offering a formula for consensus or a smorgasbord of facilitation techniques for inspiring group participation, yet there is no better introduction to the heart of secular consensus than Building United Judgment or to the soul of dynamic facilitation than A Manual for Group Facilitators.

Two decades after producing their seminal works, both MNS and CCR have been laid down and their members have gone on to other things. Yet their legacy of energizing, inclusive group process endures. Seeing the power of these books and the need for their message, The Fellowship for Intentional Community has obtained publishing rights and has stepped in to keep both CCR books in print. May they help everyone find more pieces of the truth.

Laird Schaub
Executive Secretary
Fellowship for Intentional Community
March 1999

# Table of Contents

# Preface

In February of 1978, several Center for Conflict Resolution staff members and friends met to begin working together to produce a publication on consensus decision making for community use.

The Center for Conflict Resolution (CCR) is a nonprofit collective in Madison, Wisconsin, which teaches other groups skills in group process, conflict resolution and problem solving. CCR does this by sponsoring workshops, by providing consultation and crisis intervention, and by offering written materials through a resource center. CCR works with diverse groups including food and housing cooperatives, various collectives, the public school system, city government, university groups, and many others. Although many of these organizations do not use consensus decision making, CCR has remained committed to this process as a way of increasing group cohesion, member involvement, and meeting effectiveness.

Our original intent was to write a short "how-to-do-it" piece that a reader could skim rapidly. We soon discovered, however, that to discuss the skills of using consensus in a useful way, we also had to discuss a wide variety of other group process skills. We found there is no sharp division between good group structure, meeting organization, communication skills, values, and the ability to make good decisions by consensus. They are all interconnected.

From our original project emerged a handbook on how to be the kind of group, and the kind of group member, that can use consensus decision making well. We weren't able to include everything we wanted to say about every subject, but we've tried at least to introduce some basic and useful concepts in areas such as communication skills and problem solving when we weren't able to cover the subject thoroughly.

The layout of this handbook is a scrambled montage of "main text" and boxes containing personal statements, examples, artifacts from the writing process and additional bits of information. We've organized the book this way for several reasons:

--First, any smooth, logical presentation would be artificial. We found it extremely difficult to choose a sequence for our chapters since almost every section is relevant to every other section.

--Second, we want to demonstrate that the ideas we present here were developed through interaction--a long, jumbled process that included painstaking reasoning, flashes of inspiration, argument, humor, and always, sharing and building on each other's thoughts. We can't count the number of people who contributed to this work by sharing their insights and experiences on different subjects. We want you to be aware of this dialogue, to recognize that it isn't finished, and to become a part of it. You and others will respond and build from this book, which is only an arbitrary stopping point in the dialogue. (If we didn't have other things to do, we might have gone on revising and adding forever.)

--Finally, while we hope you find this book enjoyable, we don't mean for your reading of it to be smooth. We want you to stop and think, to see comments other people have made, and to ponder over contradictions in our ideas and experience. We believe that such a struggle to understand is part of the process of real learning, and it is certainly part of the process of consensus decision making.

This book is written for everyone who has been working with consensus. A new approach to the process and a new synthesis of concepts can be useful both to beginners and to "old timers." The book is also written for members of newly forming groups who are considering consensus and for groups that may want to change to consensus from some other decision-making process. Finally, it attempts to include groups which are not planning to use consensus, but which can benefit by adapting some of the ideas we present to their own methods. While consensus itself is more appropriate for some kinds of groups than others, we believe the values and skills we describe for consensus groups can help any group. They can promote the effort to elicit the best contribution from each member and to provide the most satisfactory kind of experience for participants.

We have tried to make this handbook as widely applicable as possible. Since we believe the skills we describe can be used by a wide variety of groups, we tried to speak to a broad audience. But we realize that everything we say comes from our own experience and you may want to know what kind of people we are as you evaluate our ideas for your situation.

As individuals, we describe ourselves with the words "educator," "activist," "scientist," and "counselor." We all have backgrounds that include university education and work in academic or service agency environments. We have also been involved in alternative organizations including cooperatives and collectives, and our strongest interest and excitement are invested in the latter arena. Most importantly, we have all worked in groups—lots of groups—and we see group membership as an important part of our lives. In fact, one reason we struggled together for so long writing this handbook was our commitment to our own project group. The satisfaction of working together and the excitement of developing ideas and learning with each other was an important motivation for each of us.

Other individual motivations included:

Dear Lonnie ~ . . .

Groups that might not find this helpful:

Inhabitants of monasteries where silence is the rule!

Children below age 12, more or less, though it could be simplified and used to great advantage by the very young

Groups from very diverse educational and opportunity backgrounds, but they could be trained to use it, using considerable patience and understanding . . .

Love,

Because of the long time spent working on this project, membership in the writing group changed several times during the three-year period.

In addition to the four of us listed as authors, we received invaluable assistance from Elaine Nesterick, Education Coordinator of Intra-Community Cooperative, a network of food cooperatives in the Midwest that are served by the ICC Warehouse in Madison, Wisconsin. For most of the project, Elaine worked with us as a full participating member of the writing group. Her influence on this manual has been important and profound. Elaine left the project a few months before completion due to a reassessment of her own priorities, so the final version of the book does not necessarily reflect Elaine's own viewpoint.

Janice Kinsolving was also very active in the first half of the project. She found it necessary to leave in the fall of 1980 to make way for other activities in her life. She also is not listed as an author since she cannot be held responsible for the final version of the book. Yet this manual bears a strong mark of her contribution.

--A long frustration both with "Robert's Rules" decision making and with poorly structured consensus, resulting in a dedication to developing methods which can make the consensus process effective. "The ideals of consensus needed to be put into a concrete framework."

--"I believe people always want more than efficiency from their groups . . . They want to experience a meeting not as the smooth workings of a body of rules, but as an occasion of being with others. I would be personally satisfied if I thought our work increased the times when this really happens."

--"I'm doing this book because I think consensus is radically exciting and fun--and I learn about people and how the world works from doing consensus . . . Consensus embodies so many of the things I value. It's healthy. It's intelligent, effective and practical. There's space for stretching, kisses, humor and silence. The process/product balance of consensus pleases me."

--"In some areas of 'expertise' there is an advantage for individuals who keep their skills to themselves. People get ahead by being 'better' at something. But in consensus, you cannot exercise your skills alone. Skilled people need other skilled people to work with. Since I want to work in consensus groups . . . it is to my advantage to develop what I know and share it with others as much as I can."

--"I joined this group because I'd discovered I loved consensus . . . and I wanted to learn much, much more about it. I was hungry for dialogue about how it worked, where its origins lay, and how it could evolve. I wanted to grapple with it, understand it, and make it my own rather than to continue to float on the surface through rather idyllic group meetings."

February, 1981

Chel Avery, Brian Auvine, Barb Streibel, Lonnie Weiss
The Consensus Handbook Writing Project Group

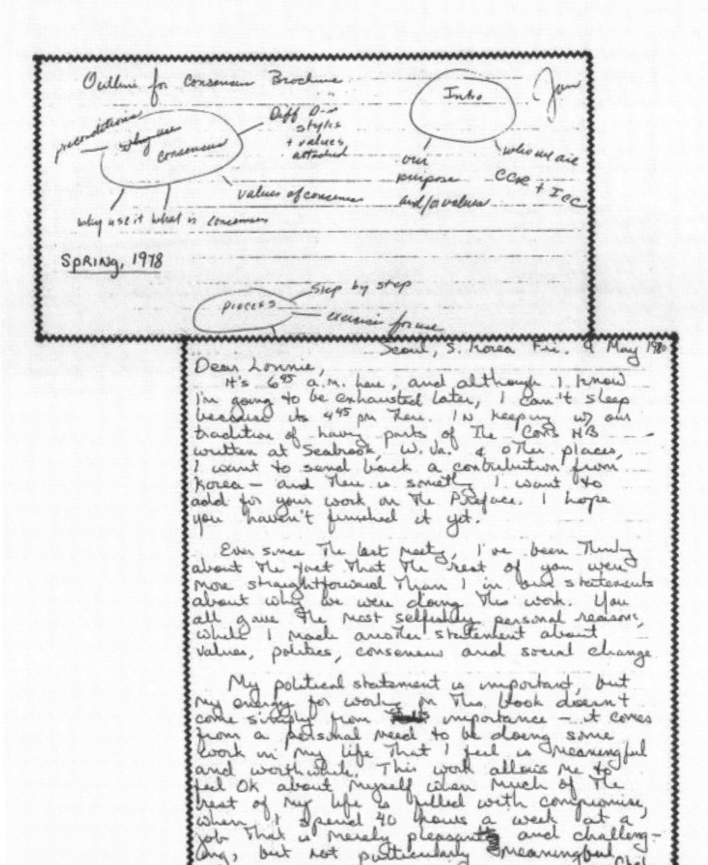

Outline for Consensus Brochure

Intro

preconditions — why use consensus — Diff D→ styles + values attached

who we are

CC₂ + I₀C

our purpose

and/or values

why use it — what is consensus

values of consensus

Spring, 1978

process ? — step by step

— exercise for use

---

Seoul, S. Korea Fri. 9 May 1980

Dear Lonnie,

It's 6:45 a.m. here, and although I know I'm going to be exhausted later, I can't sleep because it's 4:45 pm there. In keeping w/ our tradition of having parts of The Cons H'B written at Seabrook, W. Va. & other places, I want to send back a contribution from Korea — and there is something I want to add for your work on the Preface. I hope you haven't finished it yet.

Ever since the last meeting, I've been thinking about the fact that the rest of you were more straightforward than I in our statements about why we were doing this work. You all gave the most selfishly personal reasons, while I made another statement about values, politics, consensus and social change.

My political statement is important, but my energy for working on this book doesn't come simply from that importance — it comes from a personal need to be doing some work in my life that I feel is meaningful and worthwhile. This work allows me to feel OK about myself when much of the rest of my life is filled with compromise, when I spend 40 hours a week at a job that is merely pleasant and challenging, but not particularly meaningful.

...Chel

X

# Notes on Our Style

## PRONOUNS

### Gender

When speaking of a person whose gender is unidentified, we use "he or she" in odd-numbered chapters, and "she or he" in even-numbered chapters. Our intention is to avoid confusion while attempting to use the two variations equally; if one version appears more than the other, it is accidental.

### "We"

First-person plural pronouns ("we," "us" and "our") are used only when referring specifically to the authors. When speaking of "everyone," or "most people in this society," third person ("they") is used. This distinction is made to avoid confusion, not to set the authors apart from the readers. When we say, "People in this culture learn to hide their emotions," for example, we mean to include ourselves in the generalization.

## EXAMPLES

Many examples are included in the text to illustrate principles and techniques. Some examples are drawn from real-life experience and are recorded accurately, using correct names. Other examples are purely imaginary. While no special effort has been made to distinguish real from imaginary examples, it is usually apparent by the wording which is which. All boxed examples, unless otherwise indicated, are from life.

## REFERENCES

At the end of most chapters is a section entitled, *"Most Highly Recommended Resources."* The publications mentioned in these sections are the ones we consider to be the best available on the subject of the particular chapter. Not every relevant reference from the *BIBLIOGRAPHY* is always included. Full citations for the publications mentioned in these sections can be found in the *BIBLIOGRAPHY*.

Quotations which appear in boxes are followed by full citations only when the publication quoted is not included in the *BIBLIOGRAPHY*. See the *BIBLIOGRAPHY* for complete information on other referenced publications.

When a quotation is attributed to the name of an individual, the person is either one of the authors or one of our friends/associates who reviewed early drafts of the text and made comments.

## TYPES OF BOXES

We include two types of boxes: those that contain artifacts from the writing process, and those that contain examples, additional material, or relevant quotations from other sources. (See the *PREFACE* for an explanation of why we have used this layout style.) Below is the "code" for the different types of boxes:

ARTIFACT OF WRITING PROCESS

SUPPLEMENTARY INFORMATION, EXAMPLE, OR QUOTATION

# Chapter 1

# Introduction: Why Use Consensus; When to Use Consensus

Consensus decision making can be a powerful tool for bulding group unity and strength, and for choosing wise, creative courses of action. However if attempted under the wrong circumstances or without a good understanding of the technique, the consensus process can result in confusion, disruption or unrest in a group.

We have written this book because we believe in the benefits of consensus, in its power to develop strong groups and excellent decisions. In this chapter we will be promoting consensus, describing it in all its glory so you will be encouraged to try using it in your group, if you haven't already. We want you to share our enthusiasm for this satisfying and productive approach to group decision making.

We will also be cautioning you in this chapter, advising against the hazards of using consensus inappropriately. We will describe the conditions under which consensus is most likely to work well so you can assess whether your group is likely to be successful in making decisions by consensus.

For those who choose to use consensus, the following chapters in this book describe structures and techniques that can help the process work smoothly in your group rather than backfiring. Chapter 11, *TECHNIQUES FOR GROUP BUILDING*, for instance, describes how to prepare a group to use consensus. Chapter 2, *A STEP-BY-STEP PROCESS FOR CONSENSUS*, explains how to use consensus in concrete, nitty-gritty detail. Other chapters, such as *COMMUNICATION SKILLS* and *CONFLICT AND PROBLEM SOLVING* offer approaches to ongoing needs of a group using consensus decision making. These and other chapters in this book can be applied to groups that use other decision-making processes; adapting the cooperative values and assumptions behind consensus can improve all kinds of group decision making.

## WHAT IS CONSENSUS?

Simply stated, consensus is different from other kinds of decision making because it stresses the cooperative development of a decision with group members working together rather than competing against each other. The goal of consensus is a decision that is consented to by all group members. Of course, full consent does not mean that everyone must be completely satisfied with the final outcome--in fact, total satisfaction is rare. The decision must be acceptable enough, however, that all will agree to support the group in choosing it.

```
A MEETING

old friends
all their antennae out
weaving together a fabric of agreement
how much listening can a room hold?
in a sea of ambiguity
        each one takes a turn
        catching a thread of clarity
        and offering it to the rest
caring sensitive fingers
probing the tangle of ideas
sorting the threads
tying loose ends
thoughtfully
holding the pattern-that-might-be
        in the mind's eye
the skill and patience
        intelligence and creativity
        of a dozen lovers
thinking
building with fine familiar tools
in an uncharted land

                By Pamela Haines
                Dandelion, Spring, 1978
```

In "classic" consensus decision making, every member must consent to the decision before the group can adopt it. If even a single member has a strong objection to the decision (for example, it violates a deeply felt moral belief), then the individual has the power to "block" the decision and the group must keep searching for a new, acceptable solution.

Not all groups which practice consensus do so in this classic sense, allowing individuals the full power to block the whole group for as long as they feel they must. Whether a group goes to this degree or not, the emphasis in practicing consensus is on listening to everyone's ideas and taking all concerns into consideration in an attempt to find the most universally acceptable decision possible at a particular time.

Consensus is most often associated with the Religious Society of Friends (Quakers) who have successfully used and developed

these procedures for over 300 years. At different times in history, consensus has also been used by groups in Africa, Spain and Russia, as well as by Native American people. Consensus is also popular with alternative community groups, such as cooperatives and collectives, that wish to maximize individual input and satisfaction, fairness and human-ness in their meetings. Consensus decision making in modern American society is not limited to Quakers and community activists, however. Forms of consensus are often used by university departments, committees of professional people, and in many other diverse situations, often without actually being labeled "consensus." The principles of consensus can have broad applications and can be adapted to a wide variety of situations where people want to increase the creativity, sensitivity and fairness of the decision making structures.

KINDS OF DECISION-MAKING STRUCTURES

In a continuum of decision-making processes, consensus represents the extreme of highest participation and involvement from the most people. Below is a brief description of some other decision making procedures, the kind of participation involved in each method, and the advantages and disadvantages of each. Elementary as this short discussion is, you should get some basis for comparing consensus to alternative methods and for analyzing how appropriate consensus may be in different situations.

1. Autocratic: One person, usually the most powerful individual in a hierarchy, has the authority to make decisions for the group. Decisions can be made quickly and consistently since they all rely on the judgment of a single person. The autocratic method is convenient, simple, and can be effective in situations where strong, recognizable leadership is called for, as well as in day-to-day decisions so simple that one person can possess all the necessary information relevant to the decision.

The disadvantages of autocratic decision making stem from its reliance on one person's ideas, values, experience and knowledge. The quality of the decision may suffer from this limited input. People who are expected to carry out the decision may not be committed to doing so because they are not involved in making the decisions, do not understand the reasons behind them, or feel imposed upon by the decision maker.

2. Autocratic with polling: A single person with authority makes decisions for the group after asking for the opinions of others involved. Consulting with others gives the decision maker more information and a greater understanding of what other people want and what might work well. This kind of decision making also informs the consulted group members of the issues being considered and may prepare them for greater participation in future decisions. However this approach lacks opportunity for interaction, for people to think together, to learn each other's needs, and to develop new ideas out of the exchange.

3. Minority rule: The decision is made by a few people in the organization. They might be the Board of Directors, a steering committee, or other top decision makers in the organization's structure, or they may be a committee representing a variety of positions in the group. Decisions by this method are usually managed more quickly than decisions by larger groups, since only a few individuals are involved. There is also opportunity for exchange of ideas and interaction in this method. The amount of interaction depends on whether the decision-making body operates internally by minority rule, majority rule, or consensus. The quality of the decision and its acceptability to the larger group may depend on how well the viewpoints of different group members are represented by the decision makers.

4. Majority rule: The decision is made by choosing a solution which is acceptable to more than half the entire group, with each person having equal power (one person, one vote). Variations may require a majority of two-thirds, three-fourths, or another fraction. Unlike the other decision-making methods described so far, the power to decide lies with the whole group rather than with one or a few people. The decision is more likely to be satisfactory to the group as a whole because all individuals can participate. The quality of the decision will depend on the amount of discussion before voting, whether the group considers many alternatives or only a few, and whether their work was cooperative or competitive. Of course the more discussion, the longer the decision will take. Parliamentary Procedure (Robert's Rules of Order) is often used to structure majority-rule decision making. Majority rule is commonly used in voluntary organizations, unions, and government bodies.

(4) One thing you could stress in the introduction, is that a consensus decision making process is broadly used in many settings without being labeled as such. Project management, and other interdepartmental projects in large agencies, as well as corporations, are usually organized as a problem solving process. The proceedures for problem solving are well known in all administrative circles. Problem solving as a series of steps, parallels the consensus process. The two major differences are that business and government when problem solving fails, folks fall back on hierarchies rather than majority rule to make the decision; and I think in these settings, problem solving is understood as a scientific technique quite devoid of a value system. Thats probably also why it doesn't work nearly as well in business and government settings as it does in alternative settings where the value system is better understood. If this perspective makes sense to you, I would suggest including it as a part of your context setting efforts in the introduction.

## THE INSPIRATIONAL PART:
## MAJORITY RULE vs. CONSENSUS

Majority rule is sometimes held up as the ideal form of fair decision making. Often majority rule works very well. So why do we prefer consensus? We believe there are some inherent problems in majority rule that a well-executed consensus process can solve. The vignettes below illustrate some common problems that you may have experienced in majority-rule groups.

*Your political group is planning a platform for the city elections. Dave proposes that you advocate a fare increase for the bus system so service can be expanded to outlying areas.*

*You say you like the idea of expanding service, but you don't think it should be paid for by a fare increase. You want to discuss the subject more, but the chairperson is in a hurry to push this item through and move on to other issues. It is obvious that a two-thirds majority supports the plan, so most people aren't interested in spending more time discussing it. A quick vote is held, the decision is recorded in the minutes, and the discussion moves on to other topics.*

*After the meeting you and Janet, the only other person who opposed the fare hike motion, express your frustration to each other. As you talk about it, you figure out another way that expanded bus service could be financed. But it's too late to think of new ideas now, and there wasn't a chance to be creative in the meeting. You are frustrated; your group and the city are deprived of your ideas, which may have provided a better solution to the problem.*

Another common problem is shown below:

*Your cooperative business is trying to decide how to reduce expenses. Gary suggests that you cut back on staff salaries by only having one person in the store on the mornings when business is slower. He presents carefully rea-*

*soned arguments about how much money could be saved and about the cost returns of staff wages at different hours of the day.*

*Karen, who doesn't often speak out at meetings, says shyly, "But I hate being in the store alone. There isn't anyone to support me if a customer gives me trouble, and I get rattled when too many things happen at once. And on the really slow days, I get so lonely."*

*There is a short, awkward silence. Then the chairperson calls on Phil who says scornfully, "The facts that Gary presented clearly show that the logical thing to do is reduce our staff in the mornings."*

*As the meeting continues, you observe that Karen and several other people are silent and uninvolved in the discussion. No one else seems to notice or care that they are not participating.*

The scenarios above illustrate some of the problems that frustrate people in majority-rule decision making. Majority rule involves an assumption of competition. You "win" if you get the most people voting on your side; the opponent "loses." This win/lose approach encourages divisive arguing, each "side" trying to prove that they are right and the others are wrong. People may listen to each other's arguments not out of concern for the other's needs or opinions, but to develop counter arguments which can benefit their own side.

Often, majority-rule groups have a hierarchy of power in which the opinions of leaders, experts, or assertive and outspoken members carry disproportionate influence over the rest of the group. Timid individuals or people who find it difficult to put new ideas into words can be ignored in such a group, even though their ideas may be just as good. The minority can easily be dispensed with by outvoting them. So although in theory everyone may participate in majority rule, in reality this method ensures less democracy than it seems to promise.

The quality of decisions made with majority rule may be lower than ideal because everyone's ideas, including the innovative and creative ones, are not necessarily heard. There is a tendency to expedite discussions and opt for "efficiency" by settling quickly for the favored of the two most obvious alternatives. Rarely is the full range of possible decisions explored. Time may be saved, but it is hard to measure the wastefulness and inefficiency of poor decisions that suffer from lack of support, possible sabotage by the losing minority, and the necessity to re-decide an issue after a quick decision proves inadequate.

The scenario below shows how consensus decision making can be a better alternative when practiced skillfully:

*You are a member of a collective that provides training in interpersonal communication skills. At one of your meetings Lisa introduces a new item on the agenda. She says a professional association of educational agencies is sponsoring a fair for such organizations and your group has been invited to have a display at the fair.*

*"It means they're taking our work seriously," she says. "I really want to do it."*

*Dan adds, "It will be a great way to make new contacts." Several group members talk about the idea enthusiastically. Someone asks, "Won't it be a lot of work?" "I'm willing to do it if someone will help," says Lisa. A couple of people say they would be interested.*

*The facilitator asks, "Do we have agreement that we will go ahead and do the display?"*

*"Wait a minute," Lisa says. "Sara, you haven't said anything. I'd like to know what you think."*

*"Well, I don't know. I'm uncomfortable with the idea—but I'm not sure why I don't like it."*

*The facilitator suggests that the group talk about it more. "What possible problems do people see with this project?"*

*"Well, for one thing," Mark says, "we're very busy with other things that month and I'm afraid we're going to have to hustle to meet our other commitments if we have several people working on the display."*

*That comment reminds Al of something and he makes a remark. People discuss the pros and cons of the issue, playing off each other's ideas.*

*Finally Sara says, "Now I know what is bothering me. I'm not sure I want us putting forth so much effort advertising ourselves in professional circles when we haven't done an adequate job making*

**5**

*the general public aware of us. We should be doing outreach to people who might actually use our services. It makes me wonder about our priorities."*

*Lisa agrees. "I think that's an important concern. What can we do about it?"*

*The facilitator says, "This is an issue for a long discussion. I suggest we put the subject of 'outreach' on our next agenda. In the meantime, let's have a brainstorm about how to deal with this fair."*

*Participants toss out suggestions for a while without discussing them. Some of the ideas are obviously unworkable. Some are silly. But people respond to each other's ideas by thinking of new ones until a long list of proposals has been developed.*

*"OK," says the facilitator. "Let's see what we've got."*

*Most people agree that the best suggestion is that the group go ahead and create a display for the fair, but try to make something permanent that would be appropriate for different settings in the future. That way, the display could also be used where it would be seen by people who might use the group's services.*

*The facilitator says, "It looks like we have agreement here. Are there any objections?"*

*Mark says, "Well, I'm still worried about whether people have enough time to do it, but if Lisa and Anna and Rich really want to put out that much energy, I guess I'm willing to say, 'go ahead.'"*

*Lisa says, "Sara, since you were concerned about this, will you help with planning the display, to make sure it will be appropriate in other contexts?"*

*Sara agrees to the request and the meeting proceeds to other issues.*

**6**

The vignette above shows what can happen when consensus decision making is used by a group of people who understand the skills and principles of consensus and who work cooperatively together. Since the goal is group unity, rather than beating the opposition, every member is considered important and the group tries to listen to and respond to each person. Everyone's support is needed, so the softer voices that might be drowned out in a competitive situation are encouraged and attended to. Both feelings and logical argument are treated as important. When a decision is not satisfactory to the group as a whole, even though a majority may favor it, new options are explored and often creative solutions are discovered that would otherwise be overlooked.

This may all sound too good to be true, so let us emphasize again that in consensus, group unity does not mean that each person is delighted with every decision. It does mean that everyone's concerns have been considered and that group members are willing to accept the decision as a good one for the group, even when it doesn't represent their personal first choice.

Argument and conflict do occur. In fact, conflict is an important element that spurs people on to clearer thinking, better understanding and greater creativity. Although a consensus group may experience intense and heated disagreement, behind the conflict is an assumption of cooperation: people are committed to working together to meet everyone's needs as best they can. Such a mutually-supportive process is the source of this book's title, "Building United Judgment."

These are idealistic principles. They are part of our vision of a better world. But they are not just idealistic--they are also practical. Our experience with consensus has shown us that in the right situations it can work. In fact, consensus is a practical tool for pursuing our ideals--a better way for working together and a way for people to learn and change so they are able to work together better. Consensus decision making teaches participants skills and increases their awareness of themselves and others. The consensus process is a social change activity in itself, as well as a tool for pursuing further goals.

### THE CAUTIONARY PART:
### CAN YOUR GROUP USE CONSENSUS?

Using consensus is not easy. Consensus assumes certain skills and attitudes from the group as a whole and from the individual members. Since many people have learned to assume a competitive attitude and to expect the same of others, it is difficult to risk changing to a cooperative approach and to trust others to do so also. Some serious problems that people have experienced when using consensus in an unprepared group include:

--One or a few individuals block consensus to further their own power in the group or to promote their personal advantage.

--The group is dominated by outspoken or intimidating members.

--The struggle for unity takes too much time and discussion goes on and on without getting anywhere. Meetings may meander aimlessly without focus, resulting in stress, boredom, and no decisions.

--Group members become exhausted and "burn out" over time from the extensive involvement required by the process.

Use of the word "idealistic" troubles me. Don't you mean "desirable" or a "good value". Idealistic often has the connotation of "off in the clouds" - & many idealistic philosophies are quite oppressive and negative. One other advantage of cdm is that people _feel_ _valued_ by others because they are taken into account (a rare & wonderful thing). I suspect that feeling valued often raises self worth and self-responsibility feelings in people. There are definite payoffs for individuals from cdm.
FROM SCOTT

I like the xxxxx linkage of consensus as idealistic, but practical. The recognition that the consensus process is idealistic, but yet practical, partially addresses the issue I was raising above.

You may want to expand the section on commitment & satisfaction a little to clarify this point. I am concerned that some people may perceive the possibility of "intense involvement" as a negative. Perhaps merely clarify that people are _motivated_ to becoming involved more intensely in such an active process might speak to this. The essential point is that the intensity of involvement is voluntary and desirable by the participants, & therefore more satisfying and less alienating.

There are practical answers to these problems and to other kinds of problems that arise in consensus decision making. This book can provide many of those answers. Before attempting to use consensus, however, it is necessary for a group to have certain characteristics and for members to possess certain skills and attitudes that can help the consensus process succeed. The "prerequisites" listed below should help you assess your group's readiness to use consensus.

Group Conditions That Support Consensus

1. _Unity of purpose_: There should be a basic core of agreement within and about the group. Of course there will be many areas where group members have varying opinions about what is best. But there must be a unifying base that is recognized and accepted as a common starting place by all members.

2. _Equal access to power_ for all members: There should be no formal hierarchy which gives any member more authority than other members. Additionally, there should be an effort to share informal distribution of power. Ideally, then, there not only is no "director" or "president," but there is also an effort to have all members contribute and participate equally, despite differences in seniority, assertiveness, and other personal qualities.

3. _Autonomy of the group from external hierarchical structures_: It is very difficult for a group to use consensus within its own operations when the group is part of a larger system that does not recognize the process. Groups such as university departments, state agencies, or divisions of a business have often experimented with using consensus and have sometimes been successful. Their success, though, can easily be disrupted by interference or mandate from the larger structure. For example, it is difficult for a person to participate within a group as an equal when the same person is designated "director" by associated or controlling bodies.

4. _Time_: The process of developing an effective consensus group requires time spent on group process and relations between members as well as time spent making decisions. Consensus groups can often work very smoothly and efficiently to make effective, stable decisions, but a difficult consensus decision cannot be rushed. If your group does not have the time to devote, or the patience to use the time, consensus will be thwarted.

5. _A willingness in the group to attend to process_: The way group members work together to reach decisions is important and needs attention. Members of a consensus group must be willing and able to spend group time discussing process and working towards necessary changes in the process, as well as attending to tasks and decisions.

6. _A willingness in the group to attend to attitudes_: Consensus works well when group members are willing to work cooperatively and when they feel they are able to trust each other. This requires a commitment by individual members to examine their own attitudes and to be open to change. Such trust and cooperation also require a caring group community which supports the development of these attitudes.

7. <u>A willingness in the group to learn and practice skills</u> for meeting participation, facilitation and communication. The group must encourage and assist all of its members to develop these skills for the group to work well as a whole.

## Analyzing Your Group

The seven conditions described above are a tough list of qualities for a group to live up to. Don't be discouraged if they seem far away from the present reality in your group. Sometimes a commitment to reach slightly beyond your grasp can provide extra motivation and opportunity for positive growth in a group. We present the list of prerequisites as a set of goals to strive for and as a description of a strong, healthy group.

After checking your group's qualities against the list of indicators, you may find that your group meets or is close to meeting most of the conditions necessary for using consensus. Perhaps you are integrating many qualities of consensus in your decision making already. Other parts of this book will help you translate your potential into actuality. If you are already using consensus, this manual can make you aware of your assumptions and skills and can expand your ability to think and talk about your group process so you can use consensus more effectively.

If you are using consensus but having problems with it, the checklist of indicators is a good place to start identifying sources of your trouble. Are you weak in a fundamental prerequisite? Do you need to change some assumptions or learn new skills?

If your review of the prerequisite conditions reveals several areas that your group does not yet meet, we suggest you use this book to build your group's skills, awareness, and unity, rather than attempting a premature and ill-fated exploration of consensus. When you have reached the point where you feel ready to attempt consensus, do it slowly. For example, you can use consensus for a few, easy decisions first and work up to full-time consensus.

Many groups do not possess the qualities of a consensus group and may never be able or inclined to do so. If yours is such a group, you may still be able to use this book to improve communication, meetings, or conflict strategies within the group.

### BEFORE YOU BEGIN . . . .

We want to repeat that the skills and values of consensus can be applied in many different ways. There is no single correct method for "doing" consensus. In the following chapters, we will present one model which we have found particularly useful for a variety of situations. We encourage you to adapt this model to the needs of your group.

I see in your book an implicit assumption of a "consensus to use consensus" on the part of your readership. Thus I think your examples paint too rosy a picture for those readers who don't share this basic prerequisite, but would like to. *from Trudy*

In my experience consensus decision-making is an overused tool, often applied in situations where the conditions are not present for it to work. Maybe more effort has to go into intermediate steps between an organization's total reliance on consensus decision-making and it's total relaince on some other form. *from Jim C.*

Finally, we want to remind you that learning to use consensus is a never-ending process. Consensus doesn't operate like a perfect machine among a group of people who have the values and skills "down pat." Even the most experienced users of consensus, if they are sincere, stop frequently to evaluate the ways in which they put their skills and beliefs into practice. We are always struggling to do better, to see our mistakes, and learn from them. Consensus is a cooperative learning process through which we support each other in the struggle to be more understanding, open, caring and effective human beings.

## ADVANTAGES OF CONSENSUS DECISION MAKING

1. <u>Quality of the decision</u>. Since the decision must be acceptable to a variety of people, it is more likely to be examined carefully and to meet complex standards of workability, desirability, and integrity.

2. <u>Creativity</u>. Rather than a quick choice for the favorite of two, or a few, options, a decision which attempts to meet everyone's needs will require the group to produce and consider a wide range of proposals. Often more imaginative and creative possibilities are discovered.

3. <u>Commitment and satisfaction</u>. The struggle to reach consensus requires more intense involvement from group members. In majority rule, dissenting group members are often committed to the decision merely by contract. In consensus, commitment arises from involvement as well as from satisfaction.

4. <u>Fostering of values and skills</u>. Consensus requires people to consider and demonstrate such values as respect for others' opinions, responsibility for the group, and cooperation. It also requires that we learn group process skills. These values and skills carry over into other activities.

MOST HIGHLY RECOMMENDED RESOURCES

*DECISIONS BY CONSENSUS* by Glenn Bartoo

INVERT's materials

*BUILDING SOCIAL CHANGE COMMUNITIES*, Chapter 4, *"The Consensus Decision-Making Process"* by The Training/Action Affinity Group

# Chapter 2

# A Step-by-Step Process for Consensus

Where do we begin? This first chapter on how to "do" consensus refers to many concepts and skills, such as "agendas" and "facilitation," that will not be fully explained until later in the book. Yet we decided to begin with this brief, introductory outline showing how the consensus process works so you will have a framework for placing the ideas we discuss further in later chapters. Below is a step-by-step model of how a decision is developed in consensus groups. Specific tools and techniques mentioned here will be explained more fully in subsequent chapters. We specifically refer you to Chapters 4 through 7 (*YOUR PARTICIPATION IN THE CONSENSUS PROCESS, WHEN AGREEMENT CANNOT BE REACHED, STRUCTURING YOUR MEETINGS* and *THE ROLE OF THE GROUP FACILITATOR*) for more extensive "how-to" instructions for putting consensus into operation.

### PREPARING FOR GROUP DISCUSSION

A. <u>An agenda is set</u> at the beginning of the meeting so members know and agree on what they will talk about and in what order. *(See "Using Agendas" in Chapter 6, STRUCTURING YOUR MEETINGS.)*

B. The facilitator <u>introduces an item</u> from the agenda (or calls on someone else to introduce the item). The introduction should include:

1. A clear <u>definition</u> of the area being discussed.

2. A clear statement of <u>what has to be decided</u>. Exactly what needs must be filled or what problem must be solved by the decision? This statement should be precise enough to have a limiting effect: members should know what they are <u>not</u> talking about.

DO THE CONSENSUS!

Example: Vague--"We want to solve the problem of school closings." (This may include discussion of city government policies, citizens' attitudes about property taxes, emigration of young families to the suburbs, etc.)

Specific--"Today we have to think of a way to raise funds to keep Albion Middle School open next year."

C. Background information is provided by the person who introduced the topic and by other group members who have information. As the discussion progresses, other relevant information is added whenever needed.

GROUP DISCUSSION:
BUILDING UNITED JUDGMENT

A. An individual introduces an idea for discussion. This idea may be an opinion, a definition of the problem, a suggestion for an approach to the problem, or a proposal for a decision.

B. Another individual responds to that idea. The second speaker's statement is a combination of her or his own opinion and that of the previous speaker. It includes a response to the first speaker's idea and her or his own thoughts as they have been influenced by the previous statement.

C. A third person develops the ideas further. Her or his contribution is different than it would have been if the two previous speakers had not spoken.

D. Other people begin responding to earlier statements and offering their views on the subject. Each contribution builds on previous statements and yet is unique as different individuals express themselves. The effect of such a discussion is that the comments taken as a whole are greater than the sum of them individually: group members respond to each other so each statement is the unique contribution of an individual and at the same time is influenced by previous speakers.

E. During the discussion the facilitator and other members are responsible for:

1. Keeping the discussion on topic. (If it is necessary to redefine the topic, the shift should be made explicit and all group members should understand the change.)

2. Providing clarification and re-phrasing of complicated or confusing discussion.

3.. Summarizing underlying agreement and differences in viewpoint.

> Scott thinks the SCHOOL CLOSINGS EXAMPLE has 2 things going on; It may give an undue impression that making the issue clearer also means making it narrower. Clear example could be at the same level or bredth as the unclear one. For example, something like this:
> "Today we need to talk about school closings. Many viewpoints hve been expressed since we want to keep Albion Middle School open. Hopefully we can get an idea of options available to prevent the closing. Let's try to get a general list. Then we can narrow the list down and decide on 1 or 2 alternatives. After that we can investigate plans of action. Is it OK with the group to proceed that way?"
> 2 things about this: Hopefully it doesn't narrow the issue; AND it shows the presenter of the issue checking with the group to see if that way of dealing with the issue is OK. In many instances, the group must decide how to proceed on an issue.

"The power to create . . . . depends on a living synthesis of diverse elements. A meeting controlled by an individual or by a program seldom produces what is not already there in that individual or program. If, however, many individuals, each sensitive to the Light of Truth, bring together their diversity of tendencies and possibilities, something new may emerge more inclusive and hence more 'true' than any one point of view. This is brought about, not by a mechanical juxtaposition of different opinions, but by a real fusion. One may mix oxygen and hydrogen and obtain nothing new. But apply a flame and the new substance, water, is created."

Howard Brinton as quoted by INVERT

4.  Identifying new issues as they arise.

5.  Ensuring that all viewpoints are heard and understood by the group as a whole.

6.  Identifying problems with the group's process and attempting to remedy them.

All group members share responsibility for the group's process and may perform any of the above functions. *(See Chapter 7, THE ROLE OF THE GROUP FACILITATOR, for a more thorough development of the skills necessary to perform these activities.)*

F.  When it is apparent that most viewpoints have been expressed, all new information has been given, and/or some part of the discussion begins to be repeated, the facilitator or someone else states the conclusion toward which the group appears to be moving.

Example: "It seems the group is leaning towards writing a grant to the Mott Foundation to fund the school as an experimental center for community education. Does anyone object to this proposal?"

When "testing for consensus," ask whether anyone has anything else important to say. Central to consensus is gathering all relevant information, opinions and feelings about the subject, so it is essential not to move forward until these views have been expressed.

MAKING THE DECISION

A.  The group responds by agreement or disagreement. Special care is taken to make sure that any objections are heard. The facilitator may ask if there are objections, or if consensus has been reached. In addition to raising specific concerns, it is legitimate for someone to say, "I have no specific objections, but I don't feel settled on the subject yet."

B.  Concerns are discussed and the process of developing agreement, or "building united judgment," continues until a decision is endorsed by the meeting as a whole. The decision that is reached may not completely satisfy everyone in the group, but it must be one that all group members are willing to live with. If serious objections still exist, then a decision is not made.

C.  If a decision implies that an action be taken, responsibilities are clarified to ensure that the action is carried out. If a phone call must be made, or a letter written, make sure that someone volunteers to do it. In addition, some method should be chosen to follow up on the decision. This may require reporting back to the group when the task is completed, writing down the outcome and posting it, or putting the matter on the agenda for discussion at the next meeting. Record your decision and implementation plan in the minutes for future reference. (See "Recording and Implementing Decisions" in Chapter 6, STRUCTURING YOUR MEETING.)

D. If the group cannot agree:

1. It is possible that the group does not have enough information to make a good decision. Sometimes a decision must be deferred until more facts are gathered, more discussion takes place, or members have more time to think about it. Fuller understanding by each participant will increase the possibility of reaching consensus.

2. The group as a whole may decide that it is more important to reach a decision at this particular time than to make a decision that meets the group's usual levels of acceptability. Some members may feel that this is a special circumstance where reaching an immediate decision is so important that they will go along with a decision they would not otherwise support. (This kind of concession is sometimes made by individuals for the sake of the group, but a group should never pressure someone into doing so, or the result will not represent a true consensus decision.)

(See Chapter 5, WHEN AGREEMENT CANNOT BE REACHED.)

MOST HIGHLY RECOMMENDED RESOURCES

INVERT's materials

BUILDING SOCIAL CHANGE COMMUNITIES
Chapter 4, "The Consensus Decision-Making Process" by The Training/Action Affinity Group

"In almost all decisions which carry over between meetings, there is a great deal of development of thinking, and some crystallization of opinion, so that in the next meeting there is an accounting of new thoughts, opinions, and ideas. The group is often much closer to a consensus at the beginning of the second meeting than at the end of the first."

Glenn Bartoo, DECISIONS BY CONSENSUS

RULES FOR BUILDING UNITED JUDGMENT

1. Discuss the issues in the spirit of consensus: calm, friendly gathering of friends to determine truth, rather than tense contest to see which side can prevail.

2. When the meeting becomes tense, or when people are not saying new things, wait in silence.

3. If nothing comes out, or if the atmosphere is getting unfriendly and pressured, "suspend judgment"-- agree to discuss the matter again when the group can do so in a more meaningful way.

4. Take no positive action on the matter as a group until it has been satisfactorily resolved for all members of the group.

5. Be willing to repeat this process patiently as often and as long as it takes to find that mutually acceptable solution.

--from INVERT

# Chapter 3

# Attitudes and Consensus

As experienced groups have learned, the consensus process is susceptible to common pitfalls. Some of these difficulties, such as "burn-out" or misuse of time, stem from poor application of the practical techniques of consensus. We will suggest some remedies for these problems in later chapters. Sometimes, though, the process falters because of the attitudes, values, expectations or norms of behavior which members bring with them into the group. This chapter will focus on how the consensus process is affected by the pre-existing attitudes of group members.

Individuals growing up in this society are exposed to a variety of attitudes and values from which to shape their outlook on human relations and group participation. Many of these common attitudes can impede cooperative decision making. The first section below will outline those attitudes that can hamper the consensus process. The second section will describe some attitudes and values which support consensus. We want to promote these latter ideas, not only because they are essential to effective group process, but because we believe they are important to foster in all areas of our lives.

## ATTITUDES WHICH IMPEDE CONSENSUS

### Competition

American society encourages competition, teaching individuals to determine their own worth in terms of how much better or stronger than the next person they are. In a group, competition is evidenced when members try to achieve their own goals at the expense of other members. For example, there may be attempts to win verbal battles by proving that one person is right and another person is wrong. Group members may try to capture the limelight, withhold information, manipulate others to accept their own ideas, or they may try to choose the "winning side." Competition fosters both distrust and inequality as members try to outdo each other in performance, power and prestige. It leads to a focus on the weaknesses rather than the strengths of other members' contributions, to a search for points that can be criticized rather than ideas to use or learn from.

### Lack of Interest in Others

Most people are trained to view work performance and social responsibility in a very individualistic way. They tend to think a person's role in a group meeting is to contribute his or her own ideas, skills, experience and insights

**15**

and that the responsibility ends there. This perspective seriously affects members' commitment to working out problems and disagreements. It causes people to put their personal needs ahead of the needs of the group instead of struggling through the often difficult process necessary to reach a group resolution, or instead of sharing the responsibility for finding an answer to another member's concern. Participants may only feel involved to the extent of representing their own personal needs.

> Example: The majority of a group may want to hold a meeting late on a Monday night. Gail, who also wants to meet at that time, does not consider it her problem to deal with the concerns of Marian, a single mother who must find a babysitter if she wishes to come to the meeting.

## Owning Ideas

Another product of this culture's emphasis on individualism is the tendency to think of the ideas put forth in a group as the speaker's property. This attitude not only results in speakers expecting credit for their suggestions (and being offended when they don't get it), but it also means that speakers are personally attached to their ideas and take any criticisms or suggested changes as a

personal affront to themselves. Feelings of ownership can lead group members to argue defensively for their own ideas because those ideas are their own, rather than being open to improvements or to other suggestions.

## Suppressing Feelings and Conflict

Social norms encourage people to express motivations and desires in logical terms rather than recognizing and expressing the feelings that are influencing them.

> Example: Jean may argue that Jack should not represent the group at an upcoming conference in New York because the group can't afford it. Since this is accepted by the group, and by Jean herself, as a sound, specific reason for her opposition to Jack's trip, the entire discussion may be carried out at a logical level without any expression of feelings. No one, not even Jean, may ever realize that the real reason she is arguing so energetically is that she is angry and jealous. She thinks Jack enjoys more than his share of privileges in the group and gets to take part in most of the exciting activities. Since these feelings go unrecognized and unexpressed, they will continue to smolder and may be the hidden motivation behind other disputes that Jean masks in logical argument.

In a similar manner, people are taught that conflict is dangerous and socially unacceptable. They learn to fear conflict, to suppress it as long as possible, and if it does emerge, to smooth it over quickly. A typical response to disagreement is to try to resolve it quickly by compromise. By reaching a settlement at some point halfway between the two "sides," participants may bring a rapid end to the argument. But by neglecting to explore and develop the concerns expressed, they may miss an opportunity to discover innovative and more satisfactory solutions to the conflict.

16

*SAME TRUE?*

a "nit-pick", in the same vein: "conflict shouldn't be a clash of one
personal interest against another, but a cooperative effort to bring out
all perspectives"...I can live with that, but more compatábly if you
qualify that sentence by emphasizing that you are only talking about conflict within groups that have met all the other criteria (trust, respect,
cooperation, etc.)  Consensus not only "doesn't come easily" (p. 13), it
might not even be valid for it to come at all in some situations.  Some
conflicts _are_ win-lose situations, depending upon the way power is
structured.

---

Meeting notes – Fall '79.

check these top
pp + latest
draft

## VALUES SECTION.

( )

p.10. Transition needed b/w #1 and Individualism
"For example, these values include..."
General – Use of the word WE... We like WE because
its personal and it includes us in criticism/thoughts.
"1-we" = the authors
"2-we" = society – "we all"
this chapter – edit out "we the authors" and
talk instead about "This manual"
in we-2 – can edit to "in our society."
– In general, Elaine reminds us that even as
a few authors _we_ can't always appropriate
because the ideas come from the experiences
of many people.

General – We all have w/in us conflicting
values. More support/social ~~pressure~~ pressure
for one set or another in different settings.

p.10 ¶2 line 6 – change to → "We put our
individual needs ahead of others' needs and
ahead of whats best for the group as a whole."

General – final form will reference specifically
to pages/chapters ahead, rather than saying
"it'll come later"

**★★** we will work towards Barbara's idea of
Contrasting old + new values, by some rewording
and the layout. (Another possibility is a box
summarizing the contrast.)

p.11 ¶2 line 6 – reverse order of "Corporations +
~~politicians~~ politicians!"

## Relying on Authority

Many people have learned to be passive when facing issues, to rely on committees of authorities or experts to do the thinking and to make the decisions. On a societal level, this has resulted in individuals losing power over many important aspects of their lives--such as environmental quality--to control by government, industry, and scientific experts.

Listening to the advice of experienced people is an important tool in good decision making, but in the consensus process, this input must be balanced by the active involvement of all group members. When some members are passive, they deprive the active decision makers of information from a variety of viewpoints and give them power which could be abused. Members who take a passive role may later fail to take responsibility for changing a bad decision. Even when good decisions are made, members who have not participated may not understand or be willing to implement the decisions. Consensus decision making requires a high level of involvement and responsibility from all participants. Although this requires a lot of time and energy from group members, the results are worth the effort.

## Social Prejudices Reflected in Group Dynamics

Unfortunately, the perfect human society hasn't evolved yet. Everyone has grown up exposed to biases, assumptions and prejudices that interfere with the equal participation of all members in society. In one way or another, all people are influenced by these attitudes, even though they may deplore them. People generally are not encouraged to confront these prejudices in themselves or others, except when the discrimination is very blatant, so members often continue to reflect social problems in their groups without realizing it. This lack of awareness can be seen in a group that views dynamics between members as individual, personality issues without recognizing the social attitudes that underlie the problems.

Example: Sally refuses to give Abdul a key to the office because she feels that Abdul, as an individual, is untrustworthy. She doesn't realize that this opinion arises from an unacknowledged assumption that Arabs are untrustworthy. Since the conflict is viewed at the individual level, no one recognizes that social patterns are influencing group dynamics.

All of the attitudes described so far in this chapter can interfere with a group's ability to function well. As a group member, it is your responsibility to recognize when your actions are influenced by negative social training and to change those actions. You can also support other members in their efforts to recognize and change their assumptions.

My preference would be a framework emphacizing the overall goals of combating oppression and achieving transformation with organizations serving and controlled by members as means. We need to be careful about what organizations do to people but at the same time acknowledge the severe constraints within which the struggle exists in the U.S. today. Do you all think consensus decision-making is more the choice of well educated, upper middle class people and their organizations? I say this as a member of organizations using consensus. We need to address this issue so as to interrupt classist patterns and in the process learn from and work with and understand the backgrounds, needs and preferences of indviduals and groups from other areas of the society.

## ATTITUDES THAT SUPPORT CONSENSUS

This section will focus on the assumptions, values and norms of behavior that are needed for a group to make consensus work well. We describe them not just because they contribute to a particular type of decision making, but because we believe they could be an asset to society in general and to interpersonal relationships as well.

### Cooperation

A group benefits when its members expect each other to be cooperative rather than competitive. In a cooperative group, members perceive themselves as having mutual goals. They share information and resources and provide mutual support and suggestions. Participants make diverse contributions to the group according to individual talents and abilities. When a group works cooperatively, members tend to like and trust each other. There is a high acceptance of and appreciation for individual differences, and a willingness to see issues from others' viewpoints. Whereas competition tries to make me a winner and you a loser, cooperation tries to make us both winners.

One outcome of working cooperatively is that group members recognize that there is not always a single "right" solution. A group caught by an "either-or" decision may actually face a false dilemma.

There are probably other, more creative options available, some of which may respond to the needs and goals of all members. The group's task is to work together to discover which choice is most acceptable to all members. When members realize that no single choice is "right," rendering all others "wrong," they may be more open to influence by others' viewpoints.

> Example: Kay may strongly believe that the best location for the new theater is on Parkside Avenue, while other group members have equally strong opinions about other locations. But once they all recognize that each location has advantages and drawbacks, they can find an acceptable, good solution, without having to agree that one is absolutely right and the others wrong.

### An Emphasis on Mutual Trust

If consensus is to work, group members must strive for trust in one another. When you trust the others in your group, you will not conceal or distort information and will not avoid stating facts, ideas, conclusions and feelings that might make you vulnerable to the others. You won't be defensive about attempts by other members to influence you, but will be responsive to suggestions, even when you don't agree. When you trust other members, you can depend on them to abide by agreements and to carry out tasks

**19**

competently. You can also trust that others will attend to and remember what you say so you don't have to continually repeat and defend your ideas.

## Common Ownership of Ideas

An idea that develops in a group using consensus is considered the property of the entire group, not just of the individual who first articulated it. In contrast to the competitive perspective that ties ideas to individuals, group "ownership" of ideas acknowledges that new concepts are developed through the process of members responding to previous contributions from other members. What Debbie says is a combination of her private store of information and insight and the stimulation of others' input. If different statements had been made earlier, Debbie's contribution might be different.

By considering ideas the property of the entire group, no matter whose mouth they come out of, all members can feel involved in the development of a decision. When someone criticizes a suggestion, he or she criticizes the idea, not the person who expressed it. Members are open to modification of the ideas they have suggested without being defensive, or feeling personally attacked. In a sense, an individual's ideas are gifts to the group. Individuals deserve credit for their contributions, but the group's appreciation should not give individuals disproportionate prestige or power.

## Valuing Feelings

Feelings are an important component of a group: they affect how members interact with each other and how they approach decisions that are being made. A group that recognizes the importance of feelings and includes expression of feelings as an integral part of group interaction will benefit by developing a clearer understanding of its own process. By discussing emotional as well as logical factors in making decisions, the group will also have a better chance of reaching agreements that are satisfactory to all.

## Valuing Conflict

Conflict itself is neither good nor bad; it signifies only that there is disagreement. Conflict can be handled competitively, such that one side "wins" or "loses," or it can be handled cooperatively, so that the whole group benefits from the exchange of opinions and the process of working out a mutually satisfying resolution. Conflict shouldn't be a clash of one personal interest against another, but a cooperative effort to bring out all perspectives. Diverse viewpoints should be welcomed as a means of becoming aware of the strengths and weaknesses of all ideas so a strong and workable solution can emerge.

(5) On page 16, you have a paragraph about consensuses and instruments for personal and social change, which I love. What undercuts the values of consensus of government and business is competition among individuals and departments to please the "general" (e.g. whoever everyone reports to). Thats what prevents people from sharing ownership of ideas and nurtures a defensive kind of individualism, in my experience. It gets pretty bloody unless the leader takes affirmative action to nurture the values behind the consensus. That takes guts because in a sense the leader compromises his or her own power that way.

from Betsy

**20**

## Valuing the Contributions of All Members

Every person has unique knowledge, perspectives, experiences and abilities. No one can know in advance the value of what an individual will contribute at a particular time. The contribution may be a feeling of calmness or patience which helps the group perform its task more effectively. It may be a practical solution to a vexing problem. It may be a fresh perspective that comes from being inexperinced and naive in a particular area. In any case, what counts is tapping the resources of the group as a whole. In addition, by expecting and encouraging full participation from every member, the group fosters in each person a sense of competency and responsibility, and the development of knowledge and the ability to play an active role in diverse situations. This broad range of participation cannot happen in a group atmosphere where individuals feel inferior to or competitive with one another, or where some members' opinions are valued while others' are ignored.

## Making an Effort to Equalize Power

Members will enjoy their work together and will try to contribute more if they feel they each have an equal share in decision making. This equality can't occur if certain individuals have a monopoly on the possession of information, experience, communication skills, or the respect of other group members. A commitment to equalizing power means that the group is alert to and confronts situations where particular members exert more or less influence than is appropriate.

While striving toward equality of power and influence, at times the consensus group should give special respect to information from some members.

> Example: A group is trying to establish an alternative school in the community. Some group members have had considerable experience working in alternative schools elsewhere, while other group members have no ex-

perience but are highly interested in the project. The challenge facing this group is to preserve the fresh perspectives of inexperienced members while paying special attention to what can be learned from the others' experiences.

It is important for groups to learn from their history so new members don't simply repeat mistakes or patterns that have been problematic for the group in the past. At the same time, such experiential wisdom should not be allowed to foreclose consideration of new ideas. It is a difficult balance to maintain.

## THE REWARDS

We have discussed the values necessary for practicing consensus in the most favorable conditions. But why do we value consensus decision making? For one thing, consensus is effective and it produces quality decisions. In order to be acceptable to the whole group, a decision must satisfy stricter criteria than one which only requires the approval of a majority of the group. The decision is likely to be the best of many options that were considered rather than just the favorite of two.

A consensus decision is also likely to be implemented well. The high level of participation involved in making the decision will result in members understanding it better and being more committed to it than if consensus had not been used.

Consensus is also an instrument for personal and social change. In using consensus, group members practice values and learn skills which foster better relationships on both interpersonal and community levels. Consensus demands that members be more caring, responsible, and fair with each other. It provides a structure in which these qualities are legitimate and necessary. And it offers an opportunity to help each other develop appropriate attitudes and skills for expressing these values.

We have painted here a glowing picture of consensus. Our object has been to point out the ideals from which an interest in consensus decision making grows. Learning to understand the values behind the process is an important step in learning to work with consensus. The real struggle, though, comes in learning to express those values in your behavior. In the following chapters, we will try to give you a practical idea of how consensus works. We will describe specific skills that can help you put these values and ideals into practice. And we will describe specific structures that you can adapt for your meetings, whether you are a small living cooperative or a coalition of professional agencies. Keep in mind that consensus decision making is a process which must be continually refined to meet new challenges. The ideal is difficult to reach, but we think the effort produces results which are well worth while.

MOST HIGHLY RECOMMENDED RESOURCES

*DECISIONS BY CONSENSUS* by Glenn Bartoo

INVERT's materials (especially *"Short Games to Illustrate Some Attitudes"* in *"Sharing Consensus"*)

---

How about Interests? (ugly word!) Consensus works when people recOgnize that they (absolutely) need one another. Values SHMALUES! Enlightened self-interest still allows for the powerful, real, indeipensible motive of selfishness.
— from Michael

Not quite! A practical extention of the above leads one to the related principle that there must be a committment to equalizing power within the group. It makes little sense to ~~assure~~ OFFER equality to all group members if there is no attempt to make everyone's resources of equal weight. Power in a group comes with possession of information, experience, and communication skills. — yes! A willingness to share information and to provide the opportunity for those with less experience and fewer skills to acquire such is a necessary remedy.

EQUALITY AIN'T THE ISSUE. BALANCE is?

# Chapter 4

# Your Participation in the Consensus Process

Consensus requires a qualitatively different kind of participation from group members than do other forms of decision making. Two kinds of contribution are basic to a good consensus process: the clear presentation of your own ideas and opinions, and your encouragement of others' participation. In other words, you have a responsibility not only for contributing what you have to say, but also for eliciting others' ideas, even if they contradict your own. In a consensus group, each individual shares the responsibility of ensuring that all contributions are effectively voiced and heard.

## YOUR CONTRIBUTION

A group needs a large shared pool of information and opinions to make the best decisions and to meet its goals. In order to create that pool, each person must provide what she or he knows about the topic. Give both facts and opinions and attempt to distinguish between the two. You can recognize opinions by their hybrid nature: they contain both objective fact and subjective feeling. Expressing the feelings that are part of your opinions helps others understand why you support a particular decision.

Be clear and direct in explaining your ideas, your reasons for them, and your feelings about the issues. As long as your comments remain focused on the issue under discussion, you can offer new information, facts, historical parallels, appeals to group values, and other forms of argument to convince or persuade the group. Make an effort to be concise and relevant in what you say. Conciseness makes it easy for others to listen to you; long rambling monologues tax others' attention and make it difficult for them to understand your viewpoint, in addition to wasting group time.

Expressing confusion also has its place in group discussion. Sometimes members cannot articulate their doubts about a course of action because their intuitions are not yet completely formed or because they are afraid of seeming foolish. Statements such as, "I'm not sure why, but this whole approach seems wrong to me," or "I just can't make sense of this," can push a group on to clearer reasoning. Uneasiness and intuitive doubts are often the creative edge of the decision-making process, signalling a time when new lines of thought or new perspectives may emerge.

Aim for a balance between being persuasive and being persuadable. After presenting the best reasons which support your ideas, try to understand others' perspectives. Don't feel as if you must answer every objection to your viewpoint. Doing so will prevent you from paying close attention to what other people say. If you are thinking about counter arguments while others are speaking, then you can't concentrate on understanding their ideas. Each member should be open to the influence of new information and perspectives. Remember, you are working together in a group to come to a mutually acceptable decision. Make your best contribution to that decision and be responsive to the contributions of others.

If you have listened with an open mind to others' ideas, and still believe that your views are right, be firm in your opinions. A group can put strong pressure on a minority to give in to the majority opinion. Consensus offers an alternative to majority rule by ensuring that the outcome is acceptable to all participants. However you shouldn't try to be a heroine or hero and always hold out for every conviction. If you don't agree with the rest of the group, you should ask yourself if you can at least accept what the group wants. If you have good reasons for deciding you cannot, ask yourself what the outcome of "blocking consensus" will be. *(See Chapter 6, WHEN AGREEMENT CANNOT BE REACHED, for guidelines on deciding when to block.)*

## YOUR RESPONSIBILITY FOR OTHERS' PARTICIPATION

Trying to encourage all members to make full contributions and helping the group make full use of these contributions is every member's responsibility. One way to involve others is to actively seek their knowledge and opinions. Ask questions which encourage quiet members to become involved. Try to clarify statements when you don't understand their meaning or the reasons behind them. You may ask someone to give a fuller explanation of a statement, or you may rephrase something that has been said and ask the speaker if your understanding corresponds with her or his original intent. *(See Chapter 7, THE ROLE OF THE GROUP FACILITATOR, for a better explanation of the techniques mentioned above. See Chapter 11, TECHNIQUES FOR GROUP BUILDING, for ideas about equalizing participation in meetings.)*

When others are participating, try to listen carefully to the facts and opinions they present. An atmosphere of trust has a strong impact on people's willingness to participate. You can bring about such an atmosphere by avoid-

ing quick judgments of others' contributions. Show respect for others'
ideas and reinforce their validity,
whether or not you are in agreement.
You might say, "I seem to see the issue
differently, but I want to understand
your viewpoint. Could you say more
about your reasons?" Such comments
signal that you are trying to listen
and understand, thus encouraging
others to participate. An atmosphere
of mutual respect leads to a more
fertile pool of ideas and a greater
probability that differences will be
successfully resolved. *(See Chapter 11,
TECHNIQUES FOR GROUP BUILDING, for suggestions on building group trust.)*

You can also encourage other members'
greater involvement by having the group
adopt a problem-solving attitude. When
issues are viewed as a problem shared
by the whole group, then everyone's resources are likely to be employed cooperatively in the search for an
acceptable solution. This approach
contrasts with one which sets up two or
more sides in opposition to each other
and proceeds towards a decision where
one side "wins" and the other "loses."
By focusing on working together to find
a solution to "our" problem, the participants can address ideas rather than
personalities. Disputants express an
attitude that says "I don't agree with
that idea," rather than one that says,
"You are wrong." Depersonalizing disagreements reduces defensiveness and
helps people listen to each other.

Here are some guidelines for taking a
problem-solving approach:

--Before proposing courses of action,
help the group develop a clear understanding of what goals the decision is
supposed to meet, what problems it is
supposed to solve, and what needs it is
supposed to answer. Know the resources
of the group. The issues at hand should
be thoroughly understood before you
start a search for possible solutions.

--Try not to become identified with
or attached to your ideas. When you
identify with your own suggestions, you
are more likely to become defensive
when they are criticized or changed.
On the other hand, if the group accepts
your ideas, there will be much more
commitment to them if all members share
a sense of ownership of the ideas.
Ideas are a product of human interchange
and rightfully belong to the group.

*(See the section entitled, "Creative
Problem Solving," in Chapter 10, CON-
FLICT AND PROBLEM SOLVING.)*

MOST HIGHLY RECOMMENDED RESOURCES

INVERT's materials

*JOINING TOGETHER* by David and Frank
Johnson (especially questionnaires
for analyzing your own behavior in
groups)

"A friend of mine once said of a dis-
criminatory action . . . 'they had to
draw the line somewhere, and they drew
it right through me.' My fellow /group
members/, I'm happy to say, were generally unwilling to draw lines through
real people.

"The reason is simply that there was a
general effort to rule by consensus.
It's much simpler than it sounds really.
After a motion surfaces on which there
is general agreement in parliamentary
procedure, the work is usually over and
the item passes on a majority vote.
Under consensus rule, this point becomes simply a midstage. Objections
are asked for until they are all heard,
and a process of compromise begins,
continuing until everyone feels comfortable with the new decision, or
willing to live with it, without bitterness, for the general good. Its
effect is that the majority and minority bodies on any particular issue are
reminded of their responsibility to
the other's needs and desires. The
will to be together as one loving
people, when expressed, has the power
to allow the majority to give up
happily some of what might have
seemed its right, and to permit the
minority to accept without bitterness
a ruling favorable to it out of proportion with its numbers."

    by Dave Drolet
       from "A Gay Clam at Seabrook"
    WIN, June 16 & 23, 1977

---

anywhere in the whole  damn book
--------------------------------BOX-------

"May we always have the patience to
listen and the courage to speak."

    --The Facilitation Committee
       Federation of Ohio River Coopera-
       tives.

---

## TAGGING

Before you enter your thing into the dis-
cussion--your reaction, or similar experience, or whatever--try if it's at all
possible to introduce in a sentence what
your words aim to do . . . What each person is doing with speech--comparing, disagreeing, connecting, trying to get less
confused--can more easily be followed.
And the person speaking, in order to tag
what she's saying, has to look inside and
see where she is in relation to the dis-
cussion--with it, against it, her own
experience and ideas excited by it, adrift
or whatever. So there is a heightened
and shared awareness of what's going on.

---

On the introductory quote: generally quite good, and if you're going to quote,
can't change the words. But the use of the word "compromise" is unfortunate.
What occurs in consensus is not xxxxxxx compromise, x i.e., the giving up
up of something you want, a something that is assumed to be fixed and un-
changeable, but a profoundly if subtly different event: reformulation, in
which what you started out wanting itself changes. You do not lose
something of this fixed position, you change, see something better, improve your benefits in the contexts of the group exchange,the new information, the longer better vision generated. The whole nature of consensus is based on the dialectical view of reality-xxxprocess: emergent
truth, continuous self-development, and so forth. The whole nature of
compromise is based on the xxxxxx "metaphysical" (I don't like the word
but that's the one they used) view: of static reality, every change being
somehow a loss, competition, and so forth.  Gnom Michael

# Chapter 5

# When Agreement Cannot Be Reached

"Blocking" is one of the most contro-versial and confusing aspects of con-sensus decision making.  The concept of blocking evokes strong reactions in many people, although there is little agree-ment on what blocking is and is not. This chapter starts with a definition and explanation of blocking, offers some practical suggestions for the individual who is deciding whether to block, dis-cusses alternatives to blocking, and makes suggestions about the roles and responsibilities of the dissenter and the other group members in a blocking situation.  In addition, this chapter includes two personal statements with different perspectives on blocking and a history of our writing group's strug-gle to come to consensus on how to present the role of blocking in this book.

## BACKGROUND

Group decision making requires balancing the needs and wills of individuals with the goals of the group as a whole.  There is always a tension in this balance.

On the one hand, this tension between the group and the individuals can check the possibility of tyranny by the majority, a situation in which an individual or minority's views are ignored.  It can be argued that blocking is the philosophi-cal base of consensus since the indi-vidual's right to block a group decision represents the respect and power afforded to each person in a democratic group.

On the other hand, the tension between the group and the individual can also mitigate possible tyranny by the minori-ty or excessive individualism.  That is, the balance can prevent individuals or special interest blocks from overriding the goals of the group.  It can be ar-gued that the individual's right to block actually undermines the philoso-

"Blocking consensus" often carries a negative connotation

## OUR HISTORY:
## A CASE STUDY OF BLOCKING ISSUES

As of this writing, it's early in March, 1980. We have been working on this book for just two years. The group writing process is a slow one, and not as steady as we'd like. We work in fits and starts, talking and writing and going off to write more, reviewing each other's pieces and re-working them, discussing them again and reworking the ideas and the form over again. There are very few ideas, chapters or sentences that can be identified as mine, or Brian's, or any individual's anymore. We've learned and integrated each other's perspectives on consensus through the writing process. We've been building a strong group through using a consensus process in our writing work.

The single most difficult issue our group has grappled with is blocking. We went round and round and could not agree on the role of blocking in consensus. To clarify her perspective, Elaine wrote a one-and-a-half page statement explaining why she thinks blocking should not be allowed. While the others of us in the group could see her perspective and gained more appreciation for the potential dangers of blocking in groups, her stand on blocking was simply not part of consensus as we knew it. Chel spoke most insistently that the philosophical underpinnings of consensus lie in the individual's right to block.

We could agree to disagree among ourselves, but what about this book? We couldn't just leave out the role of blocking. For awhile we thought we could eliminate the word "blocking" altogether. We'd have a short chapter called "When Agreement Cannot Be Reached," and edit the rest of the book to eliminate use of the word "blocking."

*Continued . . .*

phy and intent of the consensus process by giving undue and unfair power to individuals, instead of placing the greatest power in the group as a whole.

The issue is raised: does the individual need to be protected from the undue influence of the group? Or does the group need protection from the undue influence of the individual? The individual's right to block an otherwise consensual decision is at the center of this issue.

The answers to this dilemma are different for each person and arise from unique sets of experiences. We are including some personal statements about the implications of blocking in an attempt to present the issues as completely as possible, as well as to involve you in the process of examining the questions for yourself. The story of our group's effort to hammer out a shared perspective further illustrates the depth and extent of controversy around blocking. *(See the section entitled, "Our History: A Case Study of the Blocking Issues," boxed in this chapter.)*

## A DEFINITION OF "BLOCKING"

To clarify what we mean by "blocking," we can start by saying what it is not. It is important to distinguish between the power of an individual to <u>disagree</u> with others in the group, and the power of an individual to <u>block</u> consensus. The former is at the heart of the consensus process. Sometimes a group quickly and casually accepts a proposal for a solution or action and is nearing a decision when someone raises objections or brings in new information which changes members' perspectives. When this happens, it is the dissenter's responsibility to give all relevant information, explain reasons clearly, and present the information and opinions as thoroughly as he or she can. It is the responsibility of the others to listen, to ask questions, and to seek out as much relevant information as possible.

If the majority does not change its opinion, the objector may attempt to convince and persuade until he or she believes his or her perspective has been presented in a positive and convincing way. Usually the reasoning and information behind the opinion, if they are sound and accurate, will get people to consider other alternatives or another approach to the issue. This is not blocking consensus: it is utilizing consensus, bringing to bear all opinions and facts, including conflicting ones.

Blocking consensus, on the other hand, occurs when one or a few individuals opposes an otherwise agreed-upon decision that has been developed through full group participation. After time and energy have been invested in discussion, debate, persuasion, careful listening, impassioned argument, and other explorative and persuasive interaction, after serious attempts to understand the issues have resulted in agreement by almost all of the group, then a holdout can be called "blocking."

This definition of blocking does not apply to a situation in which there are two large opposing factions, subgroups with different perspectives or, as described above, objections during the course of early discussion. In these situations, there is no consensus yet, so consensus cannot be blocked. It is only after the synthesizing process has had a chance to take place that any blocking of consensus can happen.

In short, blocking consensus occurs when one or a few individuals preclude what otherwise would be united judgment on an issue which has evolved through the consensus "synthesizing" process. Blocking is a statement of the great seriousness of someone's objections to a decision. In practical terms, it is a strong indication that the group requires more time to reach consensus. The group as a whole is not ready to move ahead because some individual members are not yet represented in the group's decision.

We continued to work on this issue in the group, though. Chel wrote a re-statement of Elaine's position in an attempt to understand it and to find areas of agreement, and she wrote out her own views, too. We made another decision, by consensus, to re-work the blocking chapter (we always called it "The Blocking Chapter," whatever title we had currently picked out for it) to accommodate all the views. "A Dialogue on Disagreement" would consist only of a brief introductory explanation that conflict over blocking is the current state of the art, and the rest of the chapter would be boxed individual statements representing all the diverse views. We as a group would present no view and advocate no one perspective.

Then things got scary. Chel thought long and hard and just about decided that she had to leave the group over the blocking issue. Her beliefs about the importance of blocking to the concept and functioning of consensus are very deep. If the book did not present consensus with blocking as an integral part of it, the book was not representing her views closely enough for her to continue with the project. Meanwhile, Elaine herself was nearing a similar conclusion to leave the group. She feared her divergent ideas were holding up progress on a project that was starting to feel like it would take forever even under the most harmonious of conditions.

Brian and I gulped hard and calmly (trembling in our boots) worked at persuading Chel and Elaine to think about it some more and try to find a creative solution. We agreed to stay together.

Soon our solution emerged. Elaine went away for a few weeks and returned with a fresh perspective. She told the group that her view of blocking now seemed to her to be the minority position, and that Chel's and the "mainstream" perspective represented the state of the art on

*Continued . . .*

blocking in consensus. She agreed that
the book should fairly present this information. We went back to our earliest
format decision to present the chapter
of text along with Elaine's personal
statement in a box. Perhaps she is presenting the view that will predominate
in a few years -- What a scoop!

The next revision incorporated much of
our group discussion and many ideas from
a longer paper Elaine wrote clarifying
her perspective. The presentation of
potential problems with blocking is included in the text; only advocacy for
positions is set off in boxes. And we
think we found the best of all possible
solutions to our problem.

        --Lonnie
        March 8, 1980

## QUESTIONING TIME RESTRICTIONS

A group of activists were preparing for
a court trial. Under consideration was
a hotly debated proposal to subpoena
a particular government official. An immediate decision seemed necessary since
those urging the group to call the official wanted to allow this busy and important bureaucrat time to arrange his
schedule.

But the group could not come to agreement. Too much depended on yet-unknown
information: the attitude of the judge,
the evidence and arguments of the prose-
cution, etc. Finally the group realized
that the time deadline was a false one.
It would have been nice to allow the
official advance warning of the subpoena,
but it was not necessary. The subpoena
could be made later, if the group so decided. An immediate decision was not
essential after all.

**30**

## DECIDING WHETHER TO BLOCK

The decision to block consensus is a
momentous one. If you as an individual
block a decision that the rest of the
group supports, you are saying that
you feel the decision is so seriously
wrong that you will not permit the
group to proceed on it. Your reason
may be on moral or practical grounds,
or based on personal feelings or on
the needs of group members or people
whom the group affects. It is important not to take your power to block
consensus lightly. However, if after
careful consideration, you strongly
belive that the decision would be a
wrong one, then it is your responsibility to block consensus.

As we have said above, you have a
responsibility to participate fully
in the discussion that develops the
decision. Blocking at the end of the
synthesizing process without such ongoing involvement is an abuse of the
power to block consensus. Another
basic responsibility is to consider the
needs of the whole group separately
from your own needs and opinions. The
group is more than the sum of its
parts; what is best for the group may
be different from what is best for the
group members individually.

When you are deciding whether to block
consensus, ask yourself the following
questions to assess the situation:

    --What are your reasons for object-
ing? Why are they important to you?
Are you thinking about what is best for
the group? To what extent are you ob-
jecting because of something personal,
or a need to express your own power in
the group?

    --Is there information the group
does not have that might change people's
minds?

    --Has the group fully discussed the
issues? Do people already know and
understand them? In other words, do

those who support the decision do so
on the basis of informed consideration?

--Have your objections been heard and
considered by the group already? Do you
need more assurance that your objections
are understood?

--What are the effects of delaying
the decision? Is it something that can
wait, or are there reasons why the group
must arrive at a conclusion soon?

--What kinds of pressure does the
group perceive itself to be under? Time?
Needs or feelings of certain people?
Forces from outside the group? Are
these legitimate pressures? Can they
be changed?

--How important is the decision?
Does it have far-reaching implications?
Is it a minor matter that you can let
go by, even though you don't like it?

## ALTERNATIVES TO BLOCKING

A careful assessment of what appears to
be a case of blocking may allow you to
re-frame the situation as lack of agreement or lack of consensus. The group
can then continue to explore the issues
and work towards an acceptable solution.
Even in a case where a decision is very
close and you still disagree, options
other than blocking do exist.

For instance, you may weigh all the factors and decide it is better for the
group to go ahead with this decision
than to make no decision at all. You
might recognize that no better solution
is likely to be agreed on soon, so you
may decide to stand aside and let the
decision pass without your support.
In an extreme situation, you might
realize that significant differences
between your perspective and that of
the rest of the group mean that you
would prefer to leave the group and
seek another group of more like-minded
individuals.

### CONSENSUS IS CONSERVATIVE?

"In some ways, consensus decision making
is a highly conservative approach. It
is often a very slow way to move a group
toward making decisions. For one thing,
no change from the existing situation
can be made unless all agree to that
change. So if a policy now exists, it
will remain in effect for as long as it
takes to reach consensus on another
policy. If no decision is reached, no
action can be taken."

                              --Lonnie

### CONSENSUS IS RADICAL?

"This individualistic yet strongly
group-centered set of beliefs seems to
result in a continuing non-conformity
of the Society of Friends with the culture in which it exists. Fresh insights
get a hearing. Any individual can
Change the group if he (sic) can state
the reasons why the change would enhance
group goals. Tradition must be prag-
matically sound, or change will occur.
Thus a certain degree of radicalism is
maintained."

                       --Glen Bartoo
                       DECISIONS BY CONSENSUS

"If people are using the process properly,
then there is no individual 'power' to
block the group--only an individual responsibility to express feelings honestly.
The power to block comes not from some
artificial set of rules, but from our
respect for each other and our ability
to accept reality."

  --from INVERT

31

If you decide not to block a decision that you do not support and you are not questioning your commitment to the group, there are several ways to modify the decision so your perspective is taken into account. You can ask that your reservations be recorded in the minutes. You can request that the decision not be considered a precedent that will influence future decisions. You can choose not to be directly involved in implementing the decision. In addition to any or all of these measures, you can ask that the subject be brought up again at a future meeting so the issues involved can be worked through by the group. All group members share responsibility for seeking such modifications so the decision meets the needs of all participants.

The suggestions above describe choices other than blocking that an individual may consider. There are also organizational level alternatives to blocking. Such options include specially developed problem-solving processes, provisions to decide by majority rule if the group reaches an impasse, or some combination of these and other approaches. Elaine's personal statement, boxed in this chapter, offers a rationale for developing procedural alternatives to blocking. *(See Chapter 12, ADAPTATIONS OF THE CONSENSUS PROCESS, for specific alternative techniques.)*

## WHEN A DECISION IS BLOCKED

When it does happen that a decision is blocked, the decision-making process does not simply stop. The group enters a new phase and members may feel uncertain about how to proceed, in addition to whatever fears or anxieties they may feel about the fact that blocking has occurred. The individual who dissents and the other group members have responsibilities to each other that define their continued work together.

## The Dissenter's Responsibilities

If you block consensus, it is your responsibility to clearly explain your reasons to the group. You should continue to communicate, express your own beliefs, and listen to others. It is important to remain open to being persuaded by what you hear. Sometimes you may have a major objection that has not been seriously considered by the other group members. Once you are convinced that the group understands your concern, has considered it carefully, and still wants to go ahead with the proposal, you may be more willing to stand aside and let the decision pass. If you continue to object to the decision, you should actively work with the group to seek alternatives.

## The Group's Responsibilities

If you support a decision that has been blocked by one or a few individuals, it is your responsibility to listen and carefully consider the objections that have been raised. It is easy for the larger group to bring the weight of numbers to bear against a small group of holdouts. Often those who block consensus are made to feel guilty for slowing down the process or causing difficulty for the rest of the group. The larger group may intimidate the minority by making them the center of attention and showering them with arguments about why they are wrong. Blame and intimidation, however unintentional, are unfair and violate the principles of consensus.

Even when you don't agree with the objections of those who block, it is important to treat them with respect. Your role is not to judge whether another person's objection is grounds for blocking consensus. Respond to objections in a thoughtful way that seeks greater understanding and creative solutions. Don't just listen with the goal of finding a weak spot through which to attack and defeat. Remember that an assumption behind consensus is that everyone comes to the process with a different but equally valid perspective on the "truth." Combining and integrating these different perspectives can result in a complete, holistic "answer" to a particular situation.

If no decision can be reached, then the group must delay resolution until more information can be gathered, or until members have time to reflect and gain new insights. Any previous decision on the matter remains in effect.

> Example: Your group has had a long-standing policy of allowing other cooperatives in town to use the WATS line in your office for long distance calls. If you cannot reach consensus on a proposal to discontinue this policy, then the policy remains in effect until you do reach consensus at some time in the future.

If there are serious problems with maintaining the status quo until a decision can be reached, the group might be able to agree on an interim solution. In the example above, you might agree that you will continue the policy only for those coops which have been consistent in reimbursing you for their calls in the past, until such time as consensus can be reached on a new policy.

## DEALING WITH SPECIFIC OBJECTIONS

There are three general methods for trying to meet an objection. A method that is appropriate in one instance may be inappropriate in another; so if trying to meet an objection in one way turns out to be futile, try another method. These three methods are:

1. Try to get at the root of the objection. The objection gives the "what"; often bringing out the "why" will lead to a way to meet the objection.

> Example: John objects to meetings being held in Farofftown. In bringing out the roots, it develops that the objection is not to Farofftown itself, but to the long drive. Further probing turns up that it is not the time spent that is unacceptable, but the driving itself. Sally, who lives near John, is agreeable to driving John to and from meetings. The objection has been met.

2. Try to modify the idea under consideration to incorporate the objection.

3. Find an entirely new direction.

> Modified from materials by INVERT

## WHY BLOCKING CONSENSUS SHOULD NOT BE ALLOWED

I hold the view that the individual's "right" to block an action undermines the philosophy and intent of the consensus process by giving undue power to individuals instead of placing the greatest power in the group as a whole. This view is based on seven years of study and of practice in consensus decision making.

In my view, the definition of blocking as an act which an individual can con-

sciously and rightfully choose reinforces the practice of individual solutions to group problems. An ultimate effect of blocking is that an entire group can be obstructed from action due to the will of one person. Allowing for and/or encouraging this possibility produces conditions which may lead to anti-democratic situations. Three of these situations are occurrences all too commonly seen in consensus groups: tyranny by the minority, conflict avoidance, and giving more power to already-powerful individuals.

*Continued . . .*

## Minority Rule

When any group or individual is given an ultimate power in a situatiion, they will (and should) use that power when they need it most. They are most likely to use that power in situations which are most threatening to their interests --where they have the most to lose. Just as the practice of majority voting makes it easy for the majority not to listen to the minority on issues which they feel strongly about and do not need the minority to pass, the individual's right to block (IRB) can easily allow a condition of minority rule on issues which are important to an individual or small group. This minority need not convince the majority or the rest of the group in order to bring influence to bear, but can merely object and block the actions of the majority. Giving individuals the right to block encourages those in the minority to take an individualistic approach, rather than a collective approach to solving collective problems. It also allows for the abuse of the "right," since it is very easy for individuals to use it to foster their own individual interests at the expense of the goals and needs of the group as a whole.

The individual's right to block is in effect giving the individual veto power over the group. This veto power may not be used often, but you can bet it will be used at the most critical times--when the issues are the hottest and the stakes are the highest. These are the times when, if allowed, individuals will resort to individualistic problem-solving methods over working things out with the group. There is also a high likelihood of pushing for personal interests at the expense of group goals.

## Conflict Avoidance

Depending upon the nature of the group and the issues at hand, IRB may also encourage conflict avoidance. IRB does not have to be used overtly to effectively block consensus. The threat of

blocking alone is enough, in many cases, to influence the outcome of a decision. I see this happening time and time again in consensus groups--much more often than the overt minority rule situation described above. A group, after some experience with its members' opinions, may begin to anticipate what it can reach consensus on and what will be opposed by a person or small group. The group falls into avoiding conflict, difficulty, or long drawn-out discussions by not even considering those options which it knows will bring about objections by these people. Instead, the group may opt for a more comfortable, easier-to-get compromise solution, or the status quo--which may not be the best decision--but which doesn't offend or threaten a particular subgroup or individual.

## Bolstering Powerful Individuals

Another problem with IRB is that assertive individuals and powerful interest groups are the ones most likely to use blocking. One of the strongest arguments in favor of IRB is that individuals who, under conditions of majority rule, would not be listened to, are listened to in consensus because they have the power to block any group decision. In my experience working with consensus, I have not seen a single occurrence in which a non-assertive, timid individual had the gall to block an otherwise consensual decision of the group. In all instances, the individuals who have used blocking either had strong personalities, had powerful positions within the group, or represented powerful interests outside the group. Instead of serving to equalize power among individuals within a group, IRB gives more power to powerful individuals.

## Summary

I think that an individual's right to block plays into our society's encouragement and reinforcement of individualism --that is, protecting our own personal interests at the expense of the inter-

Continued . . .

ests of others and the group as a whole.
It can also contribute to conflict
avoidance by providing a disincentive
to the group to get into situations in
which blocking is likely to occur.  And
because non-powerful individuals will
rarely block an entire group's will,
IRB contributes to lessening their power
in relation to the more powerful members
who do have the confidence to block a
group's actions.

As I see it, the group as a whole must
have, in the end, the final power over
any individual--not the other way
around--in order to foster working together in an environment which brings
about synthesis of opinion and ulti-
mately true consensus.  In order that
consensus be a truly collective and cooperative mode, at no time should the
group's power be subordinated to that
of one individual.

I believe that the entire perspective
on blocking should be changed from an
individual view to a group view.  That
is, instead of blocking being viewed
as a conscious individual act based on
a justified right, it should be looked
upon as a sign that a group is not
reaching consensus.  Blocking should
not be seen as a skill to be taught
and advocated to individuals (e.g.,
when should an individual block, what
responsibilities come with blocking,
etc.), but rather as a problem of the
group for which there must be group
skills to solve.

                    --Elaine

# CHAPTER 12
# Adaptions of the Process for Special Situations

## "BLOCKING" IS THE MOST POWERFUL REVOLUTIONARY TOOL WE HAVE

I believe that the right of an individual to "block" a decision endorsed by the
rest of the group is the cornerstone of
the consensus decision-making process.
It is what makes consensus different--
and better--than other forms of decision
making.  It is intimately connected with
the qualities of consensus groups:  a
commitment to cooperate, to listen and
try to understand, to share responsibility, and to strive for what is best for
everyone concerned.  And it is one of
the reasons that consensus usually produces better decisions.

### Blocking Equalizes Power

The permission of every member, rather
than just the loudest, most articulate,
or best known persons, is needed for a
decision to be made.  Therefore it becomes the group's concern to listen and
respond to all participants and to take
their thinking into account.  Not only
does this result in a more egalitarian

*Continued* . . .

group, but it also produces a more satisfied group in which every member has a chance to feel included and important, in which responsibility is likely to be more evenly distributed, and in which members are more sensitive to each other and feel more involved with each other.

## Blocking Improves Decision Quality

Blocking may prevent a decision that looks good on the surface from being adopted too quickly, before problems are recognized or before a better solution is discovered. When all members have agreed to allow a decision, it is more likely to have withstood scrutiny from a variety of standpoints. If a decision is allowed despite concerns or doubts, those doubts are more likely to have been discussed fully and the group may be better prepared to deal with potential problems.

This perspective is based on the assumption that each individual has a unique, but valid, perspective on the "truth." In a trusting group, we believe that others' insights are as good as our own, and that others will use their understanding in a careful, disinterested way. When another person, addressing a problem openly and sincerely, feels that he or she cannot allow a certain decision to be made, then we can believe that the decision is not adequate, or its time has not yet come. A better decision can be found.

## Blocking Makes Us Try Harder

When a group has an "escape hatch" that allows an easy way for making a difficult decision, there will be a tendency to fall back on that alternative "this time" more and more frequently, rather than struggling to understand, agree, search for solutions, and make the effort necessary to work through problems consensually. Knowing that a quick method for making decisions is available can result in a slackening of our willingness to try. Even when there is a strong commitment to working through differences cooperatively, groups lean towards expediency and will generally find an excuse to take the easy way out.

When group members give each other the right to block, though, they are making a contract with themselves to listen, care, struggle and to trust every other member to do the same. It is a statement of faith in the best of our abilities--and it is a commitment to live up to that best. This kind of commitment can motivate groups and individuals to learn better skills for communication and problem solving, and to question and change the values and attitudes that affect our ability to work cooperatively.

Granted, only a small proportion of groups have the necessary conditions to effectively use "pure" consensus. (Such groups are small, cohesive, and cooperative. Their members are committed to good process not only as a tool to achieve immediate ends, but as a goal in its own right since it is a vehicle for making the personal and social changes necessary for a more humanitarian world.) But to watch such groups at work, using consensus in a skillful, creative, and mutually supportive way, is beautiful. They are an ideal--an achievable ideal-- for which to strive.

Two such groups I know of can each recall only one incident of blocking by an individual during the last four years. Blocking is rare because this kind of group has learned to respond to individuals' concerns during discussion, before reaching the point where someone feels a need to block, and because individuals put the group's needs ahead of their own interests, only blocking in an extreme case.

36

I believe these groups don't just allow blocking because they have the group norms and skills to get away with it. They have become such effective groups because of the kind of commitment and effort they make when they allow individuals the right to block.

                    --Chel

MOST HIGHLY RECOMMENDED RESOURCES

INVERT's materials

*BUILDING SOCIAL CHANGE COMMUNITIES*, section entitled, *"What If?"* on pp. 32-3, by The Training/Action Affinity Group.

## HOW TO PROCEED
## WHEN BLOCKING HAS OCCURRED

It is the responsibility of the facilitator to insure that the individual's right to disagree is protected. The facilitator has several options for doing this depending upon the situation.

a) State again for the person(s) what the facilitator senses the agreement among the rest of the group to be. She/he then asks the one or two persons who are disagreeing to state their specific objections. This is often helpful if there have been misunderstandings on either part.

b) If the objections seem to be reasonable, the facilitator can ask the group to meet again in small groups to consider the person's ideas. The group may also continue to meet as a whole, but unnecessary pressure is often relieved by small group work.

c) If the objections seem to be inappropriate or off the track, the facilitator can state as objectively as possible that it is her/his sense that the group has listened as well as it can, but the person's concerns are not appropriate for this time.

d) Call for a break to defer the decision, if possible--i.e., give breathing and thinking space to dissenters. This could be as little as five minutes or as much as hours or days.

from *BUILDING SOCIAL CHANGE COMMUNITIES*
by The Training/Action Affinity Group of Movement for a New Society

*In reducing the repetition and adding lots of
examples and experiences i hope you end up with
a finished work not much larger than this one —
books on consensus scare me (as opposed to
manuals).*                                          *Ihich ⁹/₁₇*

                                                 *Early 1978*

Contents:   Introduction
            Values Inherent in Consensus
            Problems with Consensus (in American Society)
            Advantages of Consensus
            Attitudes/Headset for the Practice of Consensus
            A Step-by-Step Process for Doing Consensus
            How to Participate in the Process
            Attitudes About Conflict
            Group Building

Proposed      Methods for Dealing with Conflict
Additional    Methods for Dealing with Specific Problems that Arise
Sections:     Special Adaptations of the Process (eg, Large Groups)
              General Meeting Skills (Including Tips on Facilitation)

RE: Participation sections on Content and Process division:
     1.  Having little to say about content, and lots on process, may lead
superficial readers to make false assumptions/conclusions about our
values and priorities.
     2.  The division seems (to Crepps) more accurately labeled "I-focused"
and "other-focused" (content and process, respectively)  Many points under
process are really about content.  Maybe this sould be revised OR say
something about how hard it is to separate content and process, and how
we really haven't done it...

                                         *20 Feb.*

*Dear Chel et al
       It is great as far as we are concerned
for you to use a section from Building Social
Change Communities for your new consensus manual.
A good consensus piece is sorely needed! Tell
us when it is ready.
                              Barbara Briggs
                              for NSC*

38

# Chapter 6

# Structuring Your Meeting

Consensus decision making necessarily takes place in meetings--and to many people meetings have a bad reputation for being boring wastes of time. This chapter is designed to break down and demystify meetings so you can use them as constructive tools for accomplishing your work in an effective and satisfying way. We will examine the phases that meetings develop through, how to use agendas, what goes into discussion, and the vital details of making and recording decisions and evaluating your meetings. These techniques should be helpful in structuring your meetings whether or not your group uses consensus decision making.

## MEETING PHASES

Meetings generally progress through a series of five phases. The phases can be called "social interaction," "orientation," "structuring," "constructive work," and "completion." Some groups may find this five-phase model doesn't fit their process, some may add or delete a step, but it can be useful in analyzing your meetings for insight about where you're going and for avoiding potential problems. It can also shed light on sections within a meeting, such as a single agenda item, and can be applied to group development over a long period of time.

## Social Interaction

The first thing people usually do when they come together is talk to each other. "How's work? How's your household? How's you? What's in the works on Community Project 9,999?" Don't ignore the reality or importance of members liking to be sociable with each other. Allowing time for human interaction adds to the health of your meeting and your group. If you don't take time to make personal contact early in the meeting, you will do it later, playing and talking when you're supposed to be doing work. Socializing is fine when the group chooses to function this way, but it is a serious problem when you need concentrated effort. *(Specific suggestions for making the social interaction phase play a positive role in your meetings, instead of being a disruption, can be found in Chapter 11, TECHNIQUES FOR GROUP BUILDING. See the section entitled, "Encourage Social Interaction.")*

## Orientation

The orientation phase is the time to settle down and consider the tasks ahead. Usually an agenda is used to orient members to the tasks. We consider agendas such a useful tool that the entire next section of this chapter is devoted to them.

## Structuring

The third phase, structuring, may be especially important to new or short-term groups. In this phase decisions are made on how the meeting will function: Who will facilitate and record? Who will introduce topics for discussion? What information will be relevant, and how will it be presented? Deciding which approaches to take and what information is germane to the topic will determine who can participate or contribute. Do you seek experts in your group to guide you to your decision? Do you require the opinions, experiences, or feelings of every group member to fully develop this decision?

The issue of power is inherent in structuring. The positions of facilitator and recorder, of first speaker, presenter, and devil's advocate all carry influence. Many groups rotate the instituted positions of facilitator and recorder to spread the influence fairly and to share and build skills.

### PROGRAMMING SOCIAL INTERACTION

You know you're going to spend time on the social interaction phase, so why not plan for it? Perhaps some members of your group get exasperated because meetings consistently start late. (In some groups you can arrive 45 minutes late . . . and be just in time for the start of business.) To avoid this problem, some groups set (and stick to) two starting times--one for socializing, and one about 20-30 minutes later to start the business meeting. Another approach is to schedule a potluck dinner for the hour before a meeting--but watch out for the potentially deadening effect of full stomachs on brains and energy. Another approach is to integrate socializing into the meeting by starting out with a round robin excitement sharing in which each person spends a few minutes telling the rest of the group what major events have occurred in their lives since the last meeting.

## Constructive Work

The constructive work phase constitutes the bulk of the meeting, when information is shared, ideas explored, and decisions made. The section below called "Doing Discussion" offers concrete ideas on how to proceed with this productive part of your meetings. The suggestions focus on a cooperative approach to accomplishing your tasks. If the earlier phases have not been adequately covered, though, constructive work may be interrupted when the group cycles back to take care of unfinished development, such as friendly chatting or agenda clarification.

## Completion

The completion phase may be short, but it's vital. Seek completion at the end of each agenda item by having one person, often the recorder, restate the decision and check the final wording with the group. Reviewing the decision gives a sense of closure, can be an encouraging moment of group self-congratulation, and can pave the way to the next agenda item. When a decision has been a hard one to make, group members may need time to reassure one another that it was a good decision and that it feels good to be through it. Trying to push on to something new too quickly will only disrupt the natural flow of the group's process.

At the end of the meeting, you'll also need a time for closure, for planning the next meeting, and for a brief evaluation of the meeting or a short session for criticism/self-criticism. *(See the section further down in this chapter entitled, "Evaluation.")*

### USING AGENDAS

An agenda is a plan for your meeting, a list of tasks to be addressed. For an agenda to be a useful tool, each agenda item should include these elements:

--The topic of discussion, stated clearly.

--The action to be taken.  Is this item an announcement, a report, a discussion or a decision?

--The estimated time needed for the item:  1, 15 or 45 minutes?  (It is common to underestimate the amount of time an item will require, so err on the side of too much rather than too little time.)

--The name of the person responsible for introducing the item.

Including all these points and making the information available to all group members not only helps you plan and structure your meeting, but also has democratizing effects on the group. By knowing exactly what to expect, each member has an equal information base and an equal opportunity to influence the course of the meeting.  Agendas can be duplicated so everyone has a copy, or posted on a wall in writing large enough for all to see.

## Creating the Agenda

There are many ways to form an agenda. At CCR we use a page in our office log book.  When someone thinks of an item to bring up at the next meeting, she or he adds it to the agenda list.  We limit descriptions to short phrases, especially for familiar types of issues such as requests for workshops.

| | SAMPLE AGENDA | | |
| --- | --- | --- | --- |
| Item | Action | Time | Presenter |
| Review of last meeting's minutes | -- | 10" | Gail |
| New telephone rates:  do we want to start monitoring our office calls? | Decision | 15" | Bob |
| Update on new members | Report | 10" | Carol and Al |
| Bad news from our funding agency: it's time to start worrying | Discussion | 25" | Liz |
| Who can help clean out the storage room and when? | Request | 5" | Frank |
| BREAK | -- | 10" | -- |
| Bookkeeper's quarterly report | Report | 15" | Bob |
| Follow-up on last month's discussion about raising our prices | Decision | 30" | Cindy |
| Inservice topics for next year: Inservice Planning Committee wants input | Brainstorm | 15" | Louise |
| Setting our next meeting | Decision | 3" | Facilitator |
| Evaluation | Discussion | 15" | Facilitator |

Workers at Nature's, a collective bakery we know, write long explanations of each subject on their meeting agenda, which is posted immediately following the previous meeting. They have found they need to close the agenda to new items 24 hours before each meeting so there's time for everyone to read and think about the information beforehand. In contrast, other groups prefer to form the agenda at the beginning of each meeting, to avoid fixing their expectations too rigidly before they start.

It can be the facilitator's responsibility, if she or he is chosen in advance of the meeting, to begin preparation of the agenda. This task involves reviewing old minutes for unfinished items or topics that were deferred to the next meeting, as well as noting current topics that other members bring up. If the group is geographically dispersed and has the funds, mail a tentative agenda about a week before the meeting so members are prepared for the tasks they face.

## At the Beginning of the Meeting

No matter how your agenda is developed, an agenda review should come early in the meeting. Read through what you

have on the agenda already. Add other items if necessary. Look over minutes of the previous meeting for leftovers, if this hasn't been done yet.

The agenda review is the time for editing. First, ask if the suggested time limits are realistic. Sometimes the presenter of an item thinks it will take only five minutes, but someone else has additional information or a different perspective which brings it up to 15 minutes. In other cases, you may find that two ten-minute items are really one and the same, just phrased differently. Check the length of the meeting by adding up each item's time, plus time for wrap-up, evaluation, and setting the next meeting. Do you have four hours of work to do in two and a half? If so, you may have to prioritize issues and select some to delay until a future time. *(If this is a consistent problem, see the section below in this chapter entitled, "Working Outside of the Meeting." This section suggests ways of reducing the amount of time spent making decisions during meetings.)*

Once you know what the meeting agenda actually consists of, you must order it. What comes first, how do you want to end, and what about the in-between? You can use various approaches to ordering the agenda. By placing crucial items first you're sure to get to them and can take advantage of fresh, creative energy at the beginning of the meeting. You might want to "warm up" with a few quick items first. Try saving some big items for later on to maintain interest, especially if members' interest tends to fade after the "hot" items have been dealt with. You can vary the pace by alternating long items with several short items throughout the meeting. Related issues can be placed close together for continuity and to save the time of constantly re-orienting to new topics. On the other hand, a lot of variety might keep you alert.

You might want to start with difficult, divisive items and finish with more unifying and agreeable ones, or build trust first by tackling them the other way around. Whichever way you order the agenda, if the whole group participates in the ordering, the power and control will be distributed among the group. Participating in forming the agenda can inspire greater commitment to the meeting's process.

### WORKING OUTSIDE OF THE MEETING

Groups may need to develop procedures for editing or streamlining the kinds of decisions they undertake in meetings. A group may find decisions coming up that are complex, amorphous, and hard to approach in a short meeting period. At other times, a meeting's agenda may be full of picky little issues that swamp the group with detail work. Either way, you should consider whether some issues can be addressed outside a meeting of the whole group.

Set a special meeting, perhaps a brown bag lunch, when interested people can hash over an important issue. CCR has held special meetings to discuss the political/ideological issues that are basic to all our work, but that we rarely manage to get to in regular business meetings.

Form a subgroup to do preliminary or major work in a big area, to frame issues, to list alternatives, to make recommendations, or to make and act on decisions in a certain realm.

Example: When CCR was considering changing our relationship to a fund raising coalition we had participated in for several years, a subgroup mapped out a number of possible decisions that could be made and brainstormed advantages and problems for each decision. The subgroup's preliminary outline was presented to the larger group as a framework for making the final decision.

Establish policies that outline the boundaries of repeatedly-encountered decisions. Policies serve as a memory for the group and build fairness and consistency into decision making. They save the tremendous time and energy it would take to re-make the same basic decision every time a similar issue arises. Sometimes policies evolve organically through a summary of past decisions about the issues. Record the policies for easy reference.

Example: CCR is frequently asked to provide free services for other groups. Our organization developed criteria based on our values and priorities that groups must meet to qualify for free services. Evaluating each request according to these priorities automatically eliminates some requests and minimizes the frequency and detail with which requests are discussed at meetings.

Remember, a policy is a tool to help your group work better. No policy should be so inflexible that the group feels hobbled by it.

Delegate individuals to make certain decisions. This can be done even if your group operates by consensus. For instance, if the group can't reach agreement because members need more information, a person might be delegated to get the information and then act on it, keeping in mind the thoughts and feelings expressed by the rest of the group. For minor details and areas in which the group has set policies and guidelines, individuals should be making day-to-day decisions rather than taking the whole group's time with clearly routine matters.

If you know in advance that an important issue will be coming up for discussion, members can engage in a written dialogue. CCR has used a special notebook we call our "Dialogues Log." One or two individuals generate a list of questions relevant to an issue and write them in the log. Then other members of the collective answer with their thoughts and feelings about the questions and respond to other people's comments. By the time the subject comes up in a meeting, groundwork has been laid. Different arguments and perspectives about the issue have been identified and members' feelings have been expressed.

## DOING DISCUSSION

The actual body of your meeting is talk. Transforming rambling, unfocused, shapeless talk into directed, purposeful, cooperative and creative discussion is a matter of good intentions, structure and skills. Your good intentions we trust; the structure has been discussed above; and the skills are described below. *(Also see Chapter 4, YOUR PARTICIPATION IN THE CONSENSUS PROCESS, Chapter 7, THE ROLE OF THE GROUP FACILITATOR, And Chapter 8, COMMUNICATION SKILLS.)*

Simple information sharing is imperative if all members are to participate in decision making. A discussion can start with a review of why the particular issue is important. Maybe a sister group or associated organization needs staffing or financial help. A brief history of the relationship between your groups might be important background information for newer members. If time is a factor, members need to know that a decision must be made quickly or not at all.

Personal statements of concerns, thoughts or feelings might be the appropriate way to start a discussion. "I've narrowly avoided three accidents this month because the truck's steering is so screwy. The brakes need major work and it's eating gas like prices haven't gone up since 1973. I want to consider investing in a new vehicle."

A written proposal may be considered by a meeting. You can start with general reactions, then ask for clarification on specific points, and then deal with members' concerns. Keep in mind that discussion will be more productive if you seek positive suggestions to improve the proposal, instead of just shooting down its weaknesses.

The facilitator or other participants should periodically advise the group of the discussion's progress. "We've been looking at alternatives to Paul's suggestion for about 10 minutes now. How much more time do we want to spend on this? Are most of our ideas out at this point?" This kind of reminder can gently nudge a group along while still being sensitive to members' feelings and encouraging them to speak.

### Equalizing Participation

Meeting structures to equalize participation are many and varied. Brainstorming encourages creativity and detachment from one's own ideas by stressing quantity rather than quality of ideas. In a brainstorm, group members come up with as many responses to a question or problem as they can think of. Members are free to take risks, to toss out spontaneous (even absurd) thoughts. Safety from criticism is ensured because no evaluation of anyone's ideas is allowed while the brainstorm is in progress. In this judgment-free atmosphere, creative thought is nurtured, the full range of possibilities is explored, and the likelihood of discovering a new solution to a problem is increased.

Another way to equalize participation is silence. Taking a minute or two for silence gives everyone a chance to think about the issues and slows down interaction so that naturally quick thinkers and talkers don't dominate the discussion. Silence can be followed by a round robin in which each person in turn offers one idea or possible solution to a problem. The process continues, going around the group repeatedly, until all ideas are stated and recorded.

44

Members who don't have suggestions can pass on one turn and still be included if they think of something new for the next round.

The travelling chair can be used in conjunction with a regular facilitator. In this method, the person who has been talking is responsible for calling on the next participant. She or he speaks and then calls on someone else who has indicated a desire to contribute. This process shares the responsibility and power of recognizing speakers, distributes the awareness of recognizing members who don't usually talk much, and generally increases participation, commitment and involvement. The facilitator can always step in, if necessary, to guide the process.

*(A more in-depth discussion about equalizing participation can be found in the section entitled "Share Responsibility" in Chapter 11, TECHNIQUES FOR GROUP BUILDING.)*

## The Problem-Solving Approach

Most discussions can be seen in terms of a problem that needs to be solved. Principles of good problem solving can help any decision-making effort. These principles include:

1. Begin with a clear agreement in the group about what needs the decision is supposed to meet, and with a fully shared understanding of the issues and facts relevant to the subject.

2. Select criteria for an acceptable course of action. ("It'll have to be cheap and quick," or "It'll bring in at least $5,000 in three months and be repeatable for at least two more years.")

3. Generate a wide variety of proposals--don't stop at just two or three. Delay in-depth discussion of any one solution until you have an understanding of what the range of possible actions includes.

4. Evaluate and select a decision according to the criteria developed earlier.

Of course no group decision evolves as methodically as this model suggests, but keeping these principles in mind can help you think clearly as your discussion progresses. If your group becomes bogged down in complexities, or if discussion meanders far and wide, you may want to use these steps to organize your efforts. *(See the "Creative Problem Solving" section in Chapter 10, CONFLICT AND PROBLEM SOLVING, for a more thorough explanation of this technique.)*

## Techniques for Creative Thinking

A seminar on creativity led by Mike Heus at the University of Wisconsin-Madison developed the following four guidelines for encouraging creative thinking in groups. Try using these techniques to reinforce the problem solving model and the communication skills you already use in your group discussions.

1. Spectrum listening: Instead of listening to find fault, listen for those aspects of an idea that you find attractive. In responding, acknowledge the positive to let the previous speaker know that you appreciate her or his contribution.

## THE RECORDER'S RESPONSIBILITIES

--Note decisions made.

--Note content of major discussion.

--List ideas from brainstorms, round robins, etc.

--Note issues to return to at future meetings.

--Record who took responsibility to do what by when.

--If your style is to put more than this into the notes, mark decisions, responsibilities, and leftover items for easy identification at the next meeting. Underline in red, star in the margin, or use other symbols.

--During discussion, read back decisions after they are made to check for accuracy in the notes and to mark closure on the item.

--During discussion, read from pertinent parts of the notes as a device to slow down a runaway discussion or to return the group's focus to a task.

--After the meeting, place minutes in their proper (accessible, known) place, or type, copy and distribute them.

--At the next meeting, read major points as a review: decisions made, issues deferred to the present meeting, and reminders of assignments and responsibilities.

2. Hitchhiking: Identify the parts of what you have heard that seem to have potential and add your ideas to it. Pick up on others' contributions.

3. Use associative or "linking" thinking. Combine what others say with your ideas (hitchhiking) and blend your own and others' suggestions in new ways. Put ideas together to develop "recipes" of action.

4. Don't quit after the first good idea. Keep it in mind and continue the search for more. Don't try to kill off one idea so you can initiate your own-- instead acknowledge the first idea as helpful and suggest putting it "on hold" while exploring even more ways to use the resources at hand.

## RECORDING AND IMPLEMENTING DECISIONS

It's a shame to spend your good time and energy making decisions that are never implemented, or even remembered. Write down and verify your decisions as they are made. Assign individuals specific responsibilities for carrying out the plans. Remind yourselves of your decisions at the following meeting when you review the previous session's minutes. And figure out implementation plans that have built-in checks if you need help in actually getting things done.

> Example: The Wisconsin Drug Clearinghouse staff decided on a set of techniques to help cut down on time spent in staff meetings. To check on how well their techniques were being implemented, they chose to assign one person the responsibility of bringing the matter up for review in one month.

Nature's Bakery, in Madison, Wisconsin, has developed a system they call "Management by Commitment." They keep an office log in which are written all the commitments that workers make to do different tasks. The log provides a quick check for accountability.

A calendar can be used to keep track of regular review periods for projects, employees, or trial procedures. Post new policies on bulletin boards or on big sheets of paper in your office, and then look at them occasionally. You probably have other routines that your group uses and that you can tie to internal accountability needs.

Be as specific as possible in your decisions to make sure they will be carried out as intended.

Example: If a group of three people is assigned to research the options of repairing an old vehicle versus buying a new one, the group's assignment should be clear: How much information should be gathered? How should this material be presented to the group (charts and columns for easy comparison)? What date should the report be ready? What other factors should be taken into account (e.g., certain dealers might be out of the question for practical or political reasons, or someone might have a reason to give another option special attention)?

*(See the nearby boxed section entitled, "The Recorder's Responsibilities.")*

*The devil's advocate represents the unrepresented*

## OTHER ROLES IN GROUP MEETINGS

In addition to the roles of facilitator and recorder, which most groups use in some form, there are other roles that some groups have formalized. Some of these roles are subsets of the facilitator's role, a way of breaking down the responsibility and distributing it among more people. Some are independent roles. Like any formalized responsibility in meetings, they should be rotated so all members practice the skills involved as well as sharing the responsibility.

--The Time Keeper keeps an eye on a clock or watch and reminds the group when they are getting close to the time limit on an agenda item.

--The Process Watcher observes the group process and brings problems to the attention of the group.

--The Vibes Watcher pays attention to the emotional climate of the meeting and communicates her or his observations to the group when it seems necessary. "Hidden agendas" and unsurfaced conflicts can often be spotted early when someone is watching for them.

--The Devil's Advocate is designated to represent the unrepresented position in a discussion. If everyone agrees that the store should be closed for two weeks in August, for example, the devil's advocate will try to think of reasons why this might be a bad decision and bring those reasons to the group's attention.

The ancient Persians used to make their decisions twice: once when they were sober and once when they were roaring drunk. If the two decisions matched, they assumed they were on the right track.

47

## EVALUATIONS

The evaluation is usually the final step in a well-conducted meeting. It is the time when the group takes a look at how well the meeting went and how future meetings can be improved. It may be tempting to bypass or hurry through the evaluation, especially if it has been a long, hard meeting. But this can be a serious mistake. Evaluations often provide insight and understanding that throw the business aspect of the meeting into a new light.

Example: At a recent planning meeting for a coalition of safe energy groups, the group process was poor but the meeting progressed and decisions were made. As the meeting ended and members began to leave, someone requested an evaluation. Suddenly members began expressing their frustration with the meeting. It became apparent that some people had been so dissatisfied that they had no intention of carrying out the decisions the group had made: they had stopped participating in the decision making and just waited for the meeting to end. Without an evaluation, members would have left with mistaken expectations of each other, and without addressing and trying to solve the coalition's problems.

An evaluation can provide a needed outlet for frustrations and criticisms about how the group or individual members acted, and for concerns which might have seemed out of place in the more task-oriented parts of the agenda. The evaluation is also an opportunity to express positive thoughts, praise and support for the group and individuals. The group needs to think about what went right as well as what should be improved.

Evaluations need not come only at the end of a meeting. They can also occur at any appropriate stopping place--before a break, perhaps, or whenever the frustration level is high.

An evaluation can be either formal or informal, depending on the length and nature of the meeting. A typical informal evaluation might take 5 to 15 minutes, even more if important issues arise, and it might consist of spontaneous comments on general feelings about how the meeting went, members' reactions to the facilitator's performance, why the time passed quickly or slowly, and so forth. The more specific the comments, the better, since they will help suggest courses for the future. Beware of re-opening agenda items, though. This is the time to discuss process, not business.

*Evaluations can often correct mistaken expectations.*

Formal evaluations may be either verbal or written, consisting of specific questions to which everyone responds. Some common evaluation questions are: What went well and why? What could have been improved and how? What specific things do you think you gained out of this session? In what ways was the facilitator's role helpful or inhibiting?

Some groups write the comments on a large piece of paper posted on the wall, using three categories: positives, negatives, and suggested changes. An alternative set of categories is: content, process and facilitation. The structured approach is especially well suited for long or complex meetings and may provide useful feedback to the facilitator or other persons who were responsible for the meeting's agenda or structure.

Examples of the kinds of comments that might be made during an evaluation include: "Mary, I appreciated it when you kept reminding us to get back on the topic. We were really drifting onto tangents and we needed your reminder that it was important to make that decision today." -- "This is the first time we have met around a table. I liked it. I think it helped us stay focused." -- "We sure were lethargic tonight. I think we were exhausted after a full day's work. Maybe we shouldn't meet at this time of day again." -- "I was very jittery and edgy tonight. I just want you all to know that it was because I'm very tired. It wasn't because of the meeting or anybody here."

Evaluations are a good way of bringing significant problems to the surface, giving the group a sense of control over what is happening, and providing the positive reinforcement that builds group strength.

MOST HIGHLY RECOMMENDED RESOURCE

*RESOURCE MANUAL FOR A LIVING REVOLUTION*, (especially Part II, *"Working in Groups"*) by Virginia Coover, et al.

The Lakota (Native Americans) make no important decisions unless old ones, women, men and children are present. Traditionally, an old woman would admonish the decision makers to take into account the effects of their actions for seven generations into the future.

"Regarding the issue of closure, you might want to emphasize the importance of a good system of record keeping as a method of checks and balances within groups using consensus. Accurate records are essential if a group is to effectively clarify misunderstandings, respond to challenges, and/or revise decisions previously consented to by the group. Consensus does not imply sloppy records--in fact, it requires very precise records if the process is to function smoothly."

--Jim Struve

The disadvantages stem from deciding independently _by only one person with_
~~only one point of~~ ~~view. Only one person's~~ ideas, values, experience and knowledge ~~are considered.~~
The quality of the decision may suffer from lack of access to other's _information,_
and ~~if the~~ ~~people are expected to carry the decision out they may not be~~
~~highly committed to it since their viewpoints weren't considered and since they may~~ _weren't_
~~involved in the decision. They may not understand why the decision is necessary,~~
~~not know the reasoning behind the decision. and they feel imposed on by the decision.~~

2) **Autocratic with Polling:** A single person _with authority_ makes the decision after asking

for the opinions of others involved. ~~This method allows some opportunity to~~
_Consulting with others_
~~include~~ the ideas of more people and ~~involves~~ the decision maker a feeling of

what people want. ~~But there is still~~ no opportunity for interaction, for people to

think together, learn each other's needs, and perhaps develop new ideas out of the
_This form of decision making is a good transition from_
exchange. ~~autocratic do group forms of decision making. It does, however, lack~~

3) **Minority Rule:** The decision is made by a few people. They might be the
_top decision makers in the_
Board of Directors, a Steering Committee, or others ~~at the top of the hierarchy.~~ _hierarchy._
~~Minority rule may~~ committee representing a variety of positions in the group.

~~method usually~~ ~~than~~ decisions by larger groups, since only a

few individuals are involved. There is some opportunity for interaction here.

~~workings~~ The quality of the decision and its acceptability to the group may depend

on how well the viewpoints of different group members were represented by the

decision makers.

4) **Majority Rule:** The decision is made by choosing a solution which is

acceptable to more than half of the entire group with each person having equal

~~one vote).~~ Variations may require a majority of two-thirds,

~~decision-making methods described so far~~

most "democratic" since

more likely to be satisfactory to the group as a whole.

~~appropriate~~ the decision will depend on the amount of inter-

had before voting. Of course the more discussion, the longer the

~~ske.~~ Parliamentary Procedure or Roberts' Rules of Order are often

structure majority rule decision making.

Chapter 7

# The Role of the Group Facilitator

## WHAT IS A FACILITATOR?

To facilitate means "to make easy."
The group facilitator's job is to make
it easier for the group to do its work.
By providing non-directive leadership,
the facilitator helps the group arrive
at the understandings and decisions
that are its task.  In a consensus group
the facilitator's focus is on the group
and its work.  The role is one of assistance and guidance, not of control.

A group needs facilitation in both the
content and the process of its work.
Content facilitation includes clarifying confusing statements, identifying
themes or common threads in a discussion,
summarizing and organizing the ideas
put forth, and "testing for consensus"
by expressing the decisions that appear
to emerge from the group process.  These
functions focus on what the group is
talking about.  Process functions, on
the other hand, relate to how the group
is working.  They include making sure
everyone gets a chance to participate,
pointing out feelings that are interfering with the group's work, and helping members to express and deal with
their conflicts.  Content and process
are both vital and basic elements to
achieving the group's purpose.

To guide a group well calls for careful
observation and attention.  In addition
to listening closely to what people are
saying, the facilitator should watch
participants' faces and posture for nonverbal cues on how the process is working.  Eye contact can be used to acknowledge people's wishes to speak and
to let them know their ideas are being
heard.  When facilitating, you must pay
full attention throughout the meeting in
an attempt to understand what is going
on.

The group facilitator should abstain
from participation in partisan discussions.  Good facilitation is hard work
and it is difficult, if not impossible,
to attend to the group's dynamics and
needs as well as to your personal wish
to urge a particular point.  A little
distance is important for keeping the
whole picture in view and to guide the
group toward its goals.

## SHARING FACILITATION

The facilitator's job is to be sure
that all the facilitation functions are
filled--but not necessarily to do it all
him or herself.  All group members share
the responsibility and skills for
achieving the meeting's purpose.  When

the process becomes particularly difficult, you might say, "I'm having a hard time now. I want help finding a common thread," or "Can someone summarize where we are now? We've been all over the map on this issue and I'm confused about how to proceed."

Another way to share facilitation is to step out of the role for part of the meeting when you want to be actively involved in the topic being discussed. It is the responsibility of both the facilitator and the group to notice when a different person should be facilitating. "I have some strong feelings about this subject and it's hard to be objective, plus I want to be able to participate. Will someone else facilitate for now?" -- "Henry, you're getting involved in this and no one is really facilitating now. Is there someone else who's not so connected to this issue who can step in and facilitate for awhile?"

Many groups use team facilitation as a way to ease the responsibility on one person and to allow beginners to gradually gain experience and confidence. Effective team facilitation takes practice and good feedback from other members. *(Ideas about sharing the facilitator's functions are suggested in*

*Chapter 6, STRUCTURING YOUR MEETINGS, in a box entitled, "Other Roles in Group Meetings." Also see the section "Formalized Process" in Chapter 12, ADAPTATIONS OF THE PROCESS FOR SPECIAL SITUATIONS.)*

## FACILITATIVE FUNCTIONS

The rest of this chapter describes specific functions and techniques a facilitator and all group members can use, presented in a roughly chronological order. Although some points relate directly to content and others address explicitly process aspects of a meeting, we have not attempted to separate content from process functions since in practice there is often some overlap between the two. Similarly, we have not completely eliminated the overlap among the functions themselves. Illustrations of one technique may also apply to another.

There is no single "right" way to perform these functions in a meeting, and no one person is ever so accomplished in all of these skills that he or she can perform them all at once. Different people develop their own unique styles of meeting facilitation and make different kinds of contributions in the role. By recognizing and appreciating this fact, groups can encourage and help their members to improve their facilitation skills while calling on the special abilities that individuals have when they are needed in special situations.

Example: Thea and Pete may be asked to co-facilitate a difficult meeting because Thea is very good at keeping the group focused and moving towards its goal, while Pete's best ability is to sharpen conflict and help people express their feelings. As a team, they complement each other and can learn from each other.

Whether you are acting in the role of facilitator or not, the skills described below can help you improve your contribution in a meeting.

52

Example: "We've got several short
items under five minutes each, plus
three fifteen-minute ones, plus the
big membership discussion that we
need at least an hour for. I suggest that we get to as many of the
shorties as we can in half an hour,
then do the membership thing, and
then do the three other items after
a break. Is that all right with
everybody? OK, are there any short
ones that we absolutely have to get
to tonight, that we should start
off with?"

The facilitator in this case offers
direction, but the suggestions must be
affirmed or altered by the group.

As the meeting progresses, the facilitator keeps track of where the group is
on the planned agenda, monitors the
time, and gives this information to the
group periodically. *(See "Using Agendas"
in Chapter 6, STRUCTURING YOUR MEETINGS.")*

## Keeping the Discussion on Topic

Since most issues have many facets and
ramifications, and bring related topics
to participants' inquisitive minds, it
is common to get sidetracked or to go
into unnecessary detail on an issue.
The facilitator should be aware of this
tendency and be ready to help the discussion get back on track. The importance of this function is a major reason
that the facilitator should remain
neutral and not participate in hot debates.

The facilitator (or anyone) who notices
that the group discussion has shifted
from the original intent can interrupt
with comments like "I think we've
wandered away from our focus." --
"How does what we're talking about here
relate to the logo design question we
started on?" -- "These are good ideas
for a silkscreen technique, but we're
not ready for that until we decide on
the logo. Let's get back to that."
At such times, the facilitator has the
responsibility to interrupt the dis-

## Guiding the Agenda

The facilitator or another member may
begin the meeting. If the group cus-
tomarily begins with a short check-in
period, introductions to new attenders,
or some way of greeting each other
personally, that should be done first.
"Does anyone feel like starting the
check-in?"

The first order of business is to introduce the agenda, whether it is posted on
the wall, copied for everyone, or in the
facilitator's hands. The facilitator
should read the agenda items aloud, ask
for time assignments if they are not
already clear, and add, eliminate, and
set priorities among the items. The
agenda review orients the group to the
tasks at hand.

The facilitator should conduct the
agenda review quickly but thoroughly.
A clear summary may be appropriate.

cussion and even an individual. Be gentle but firm, and use eye contact to make a friendly connection with the person you cut off.

Sometimes members get so involved in an issue that they lose sight of the group's goal for the discussion. For example, Tina may want to share her knowledge and excitement about computer systems while the group only needs information about one specific concept. To avoid lost time and frustration, it helps to have clearly defined goals for all discussions (to explore, to decide, to design) and to remind the group of these goals. Members can often correct themselves if given a gentle reminder.

## Clarifying and Rephrasing

The facilitator may act as a translator if members are not being well understood. This skill may be called for if members are talking past each other and not understanding each other's points, and if feelings are rising as the miscommunication continues. One tool in such situations is to rephrase the difficult points.

> Example: "I think Luan's point is that the city funding simply may not be available next year, aside from other problems with that funding. Have I understood you right, Luan?"

Be sure to check your interpretation with the speaker for accuracy.

When things get muddled or confused, re-define (or have someone else re-define) the topic clearly.

> Example: "It seems that we're talking about why we really want group T-shirts and who'll pay for them, and we have to consider these things before we can get into the question of who will do the art work."

Always get group acceptance of the re-definition.

Clarification can be helpful throughout the course of group discussion. It can improve group members' understanding of individual opinions as well as of the issues at hand, and it can save time that might otherwise be lost to confused and unnecessary interaction that is based on misunderstanding.

## Equalizing Participation

The facilitator should be aware of who is speaking repeatedly and who is not speaking at all, in order to help equalize members' participation. Some members may speak more or less than others for a variety of reasons: their interest and involvement in the subject, their knowledge of the issues, their confidence in speaking in groups, their self concept as affected by age, sex, social class background, and so forth. Try to be sensitive to the impact of members' personal histories on their participation.

A variety of techniques are available for facilitators to use in equalizing participation and encouraging full involvement of all members in discussions. The most direct approach is

GENERAL COMMENTS ON EXAMPLES:

Find and use more examples with less than opitmal/perfect/pie in the sky outcomes. (P.26/a-c is "in the clouds")

Do the examples skew things about men's roles in groups? Joe thinks perhaps men come across as "bad guys" more often than women, maybe more often than is realistic.

**54**

to simply ask silent members if they have anything to say and request over-participating, dominating members to refrain from speaking at times.

> Example: "Excuse me, Jim, but we've heard several of your thoughts on this already. Carol hasn't spoken yet and it looks like she's got something to add. Carol?"

> Or: "We've heard from many of the men in the group. Let's hear from the women, too."

Other techniques for equalizing participation include structural procedures such as round robins, brainstorms, etc. *(See the "Share Responsibility" section in Chapter 11, TECHNIQUES FOR GROUP BUILDING.)*

*Consensus takes time and patience*

## Pacing

A subtle but important function of the facilitator is to pace the meeting. A good group discussion moves at a comfortable tempo, neither too slowly so the meeting drags and people get bored and listless, nor too fast, leaving members feeling anxious, confused or left out. Pacing requires maintaining the delicate balance between allowing enough time for the group to discuss and understand an issue adequately, and letting the group get bogged down in too much detail.

You can slow down the pace of a heated meeting by asking for a moment of silence, or by suggesting, "This is moving too fast for me. Let's slow it down a bit." If a speedy discussion appears to be ending too soon, you can say, "I think we need to spend a little more time on this. Did some of the others here have any comments or questions to add?"

You can speed up the pace by advising the group of the time or requesting that people move along. "We've spent fifteen minutes on this now. How much time do we want to give it?" Even sitting up straighter and showing more energy in your body can have an effect.

## Reformulating

One of the most important functions a facilitator can perform is called reformulating. This function goes a step further than clarifying, and is useful when many issues or points of conflict evolve out of a discussion on a single topic. The first step in reformulation is to separate the areas of agreement from the areas of disagreement. Ask the group for acceptance of what you perceive to be an area of agreement. If it is accepted and is part of the decision to be made, record it and set it aside. Then go on to discuss the area of disagreement, and do the same until consensus is reached.

> Example: Susan requested that CCR allow her to spend about $50 to purchase layout materials for our newsletter production. After a fairly detailed discussion we found, by separating the issues, that we were in agreement about everything except one item. Roger thought we could build a layout board ourselves easily and more cheaply. But by excluding this item from the discussion, we were able to reach agreement that Susan could purchase the other materials.

**55**

In the course of seemingly endless debate, the process of pointing out areas of agreement can remind members of their common ideas and can bring people together even in the face of intense disagreement on other matters. Clarifying the areas of disagreement sharpens the focus of group discussion. It helps members know what the real issues are and what particular problems have to be solved.

Another function of reformulation is to identify new issues as they arise and bring them to the group's attention. Whenever a new issue is raised, the group should consider what to do with it. If it is more important and fundamental than the issue being discussed originally, perhaps it should take precedence and be addressed first. It may belong further down on the present agenda, or it could just be dropped, if unimportant. The facilitator might ask, "Can we put this on the agenda for the next meeting?" Or you might suggest, "It's clear to me that we must address our basic goals before continuing with the original discussion." Or, "I think we should come back to this later, OK?"

> Example: During an agency staff meeting, Sara requested a two-week vacation during the next month. The tense and difficult discussion in response to her request brought out a separate problem. Vacation time policy was unclear, other staff did not request as much time away as Sara, and there were strong feelings of resentment. The issue of Sara's vacation request was reformulated as a problem of vague and uncertain expectations among the staff. The group decided to give Sara her vacation, but to address the need to develop a policy about vacation time. They also decided to begin a policy book to help standardize work-related expectations among the staff.

## A CASE OF REFORMULATION

A few years ago at CCR we found ourselves with 17 members, after being accustomed to a size of nine to 12. We decided to address the problem of size. Soon we were expressing many feelings about the group, our access to one another, the way work was being done, and our roles and goals for the group. Eventually we reformulated our problem as one of structure, not of size. "Are we agreed that although we want to keep our present membership, we're not satisfied with how the group is working and therefore we need to change parts of our structure to fit the larger group size?" Size was where we started, but we found the solution to our problem along a different dimension.

## Identifying Interpersonal Communication Problems

Be aware of the quality of communication between members. If you perceive, for example, that one member is not listening to another member's opinion, which in turn is contributing to difficulty in achieving consensus, point this out. "Jan, please listen to Elaine. I don't think you're getting her point." You may also help by rephrasing a thought, or asking a person to rephrase their previous statements. Then ask whether others understood the restatement, or have any questions. "May, I think that is an important issue. Can you say that again, in another way, to make sure everyone is clear on the point?" Having speakers rephrase each other's positions is another quick way to check for understanding. "Jon, can you say what you understand Lou to be saying . . . Lou, can you say back what you hear?" If you recognize that a problem exists, but do not have immediate solutions, ask the group for help. "Can someone help Jon and Lou see what the other is saying?" *(See Chapter 8, COMMUNICATION SKILLS, for more suggestions.)*

## Summarizing

The direction and pace of a meeting are helped by the occasional interjection of summarizing statements from the facilitator or other group members. Summaries help bring issues into perspective; they allow the group to see a direction to the discussion, to refocus the discussion on the topic, or to test how close to decision they really are. A summary might be: "So, I hear us saying that we support the idea of staying open till 9:00 p.m. on Wednesdays, and we still have to deal with Jeff and Karla's concerns about phone coverage."

Summarizing also helps to pace or move a meeting along. Good summaries can often help members realize they have actually reached agreement in a discussion that seemed complicated and unresolvable. Of course, any summary might be incorrect or misplaced in emphasis, in which case the group should object and correct the summary statement.

## Aiding the Group's Emotional Climate

The facilitator should be conscious of the emotional atmosphere of the group. Do members seem listless and depressed? Is excitement high but unfocused, perhaps spilling over into unproductive highjinks? Just keeping track of the group's mood is important, but you can also use the facilitation role to make positive and constructive changes in the atmosphere. Good pacing is one way of maintaining a positive group atmosphere. Other possibilities include a break when members are restless, a quick energizing activity when they can't concentrate anymore, or a moment of silence when an argument is so heated that participants aren't listening to one another. *(See Chapter 9, WORKING WITH EMOTIONS, for more general discussion on this topic. Also see the section, "Encourage Social Interaction," in Chapter 11, TECHNIQUES FOR GROUP BUILDING.)*

In difficult situations, it can be helpful to remind members of what the consensus process requires--qualities such as active listening, being open to influence by others, or focusing on the problem instead of on personalities. Such a comment can provide guidance and perspective and can re-orient the members to the group's goals.

> Example: "People, this discussion is hard, but I think we're doing pretty well at listening to one another. Let's remain clear that the problem is what to do about the law suit, not whether Johnny or Claire has a better approach."

A reminder of just what needs to be accomplished and what the group has in common may pull people out of their negative feelings or their attachment to their own ideas and back to constructive work.

*Dangerous to offer ppl the end product of our process as "oughts." Give guidelines to develop their own process.*

## Identifying Individual Emotions as They Arise

When individual emotions interfere with the group's decision-making process, it's often useful to take time to identify and respond to them. If she looks like she is about to cry, you could say, "Debby, you look upset about what Dan said. Do you want to talk about it?" Use your judgment and intuition in choosing who, when, and how much to delve into individual's emotions. Is this feeling an important one to concern the group with? Does it greatly affect the group's dynamics or the group's understanding of an issue, or the reaching of consensus? Does the member probably need recognition and a response, or would he or she dislike being made the center of attention? *(Refer to Chapter 9, WORKING WITH EMOTIONS, for further discussion of the role of emotions in group process.)*

## Conflict Management

Conflict and disagreement are a natural, necessary, and potentially creative part of group interaction. Disagreement and criticism, though, should always be focused on ideas, issues and behaviors, not on members' personhood. No one should ever be personally attacked. In new groups, the facilitator should state this as a guideline from the start. When it happens, the facilitator should interrupt the attack and help the people re-focus on the issues.

Sometimes the absence of visible conflict among group members can be an even greater problem, especially if this is a pattern of interaction within the group. Many groups perceive lack of conflict as an indication of agreement or good meeting process. "Niceness," though, can prevent real disagreement from being expressed, leaving it to fester under the surface. If you think that conflict is being suppressed, try to bring it out. "I sense that we're not addressing all the issues." -- "In my experience, it is unusual to find total agreement on a subject as important as this. I suspect there's more here than people are saying so far."

Identify what you perceive to be disagreement, or ask questions to find out whether people do agree. Raise or delve into points which may bring out the disagreement. If the tension is high but people aren't talking, a simple, "What's going on here?" might open things up. Try these tactics when you suspect the group is suppressing an important issue, but don't chase conflict for its own sake.

Once conflict is out in the open, try to help members see all the perspectives on the issue. Using a "round robin" gives everyone a chance to speak without fearing argumentative response. To help people see different perspectives, you might ask someone to play devil's advocate, or suggest that individuals reverse roles and argue the opinions opposite to their own. *(See Chapter 10, CONFLICT AND PROBLEM SOLVING, for more about structural approaches to conflict. See Chapter 8, COMMUNICATION SKILLS, for more about improving communication when the risks of misunderstanding are high.)*

## Testing for Agreement

A function that is closely related to summarizing, but more specific and focused, is testing for agreement. When you think that agreement may be close, clearly ask the group if they do, in fact, agree. Ask, "Does everyone agree that . . . ?" -- "My sense is that we have agreement in . . ." -- "Are there any objections to the proposal that . . . ?" When you test for agreement, do so in a tentative way that leaves room for input, correction and disagreement as well as for affirmation. And be sure to fully state the proposal that you are testing. Don't assume that everyone knows what it is because Jack explained it three minutes ago.

## Soliciting Feedback

Getting feedback is fundamental to everything the facilitator does. Although you are responsible for keeping the direction and focus of the discussion in perspective, and are active in guiding that direction and focus, the direction itself is always received from the group. As facilitator, you speak for the group and need endorsement for doing so.

As facilitator, you should regularly ask for acceptance, feedback, agreement or disagreement on your rephrasing, clarification, redefinition, summary and reformulation statements, and finally on your reflection of the "sense of the meeting." We're all human and there's no such thing as true objectivity. Despite the best efforts, you could subtly bend things in the direction of your own opinions, or you might simply misjudge the sense of the group. It's important for the group to reject such statements if they're incorrect.

It is extremely valuable to set a tone in the group of openness, with the expectation that the group monitors the facilitator. Let people know that it is their responsibility to disagree with you. "I'm going to call 'em as I see 'em, so if you see things differently, please say so right away. My interpretation isn't necessarily right." This tone setting is ideal, if the group can follow through with it, because it can be deadly boring for the facilitator to be constantly asking for group approval for his or her interpretations. Find a balance between an overly confident, cavalier approach and an uncertain, wimpy one.

## Decision Identification and Implementation

Once a decision is made, the facilitator should make sure that everyone understands what it is and what it is not. Make sure it gets recorded. If there is any possibility of doubt, have the note taker read it back to the group to ensure clarity. Also make sure the group decides how the decision will be carried out. Who will take responsibility to see that it is done? By when will it be done? What are the criteria for knowing it has been done? What kind of review or follow-up is necessary and when will this happen? (See the section entitled, "Recording and Implementing Decisions," in Chapter 6, STRUCTURING YOUR MEETINGS.)

---

COMPONENTS OF DECISIONS

--What exactly is the decision?

--Who is going to do it?

--What information and/or materials do they need to do it?

--By when will it be done?

--How will the group know it has been done?

## MOST HIGHLY RECOMMENDED RESOURCES

*A MANUAL FOR GROUP FACILITATORS* by Brian
  Auvine, et al.

*"Leadership for Change"* by Bruce Kokopeli
  and George Lakey

*"Meeting Facilitation: The No-Magic
  Method"* by Berit Lakey

---

For Michel

__Introduction__   Suggestions and Comments

① An initial "who we are" at CCR or FCR, and some legitimation of our use of consensus. It would be nice to link it with the definition of consensus in the 1st paragraph. Otherwise, it could be a separate note, "Let us introduce ourselves"

② Re definition at beginning "... kind of democratic decision-making process"!

③ Can further legitimize consensus decision-making in paragraph? "It has also been used successfully by university depts., groups of professional people, civic organizations, and a variety of groups too numerous to mention. etc. etc."

After we say who has used it successfully, how about a statement stressing strongly that we believe it can work for you too ...

④ Switch pts. #1 + #2 (p.2) maybe since skills and tangibles usually get fewer, whereas "emotions" are more harder hardest difficult to "own"

⑤ On page 3 where you store suggests, it might be clearer if they are ... Goals + outcome goals, "what we will be talking about in this pamphlet is ..." and "Through practice + reading once you should be able to do ..." Not in those exact words of course.

I like the blending of culture + skills. Other than recommending of things, that's all I can think of. I think it's great you worked on it Sentence.

— Sunion

Dear Jan, Bob, Elaine & Brian —
  I'm sitting on the floor of a kitchen in New Hampshire with my back against a radiator — so there are limits to how much I can do. Below are just some ideas for what might go into The Introduction. Some of The stuff probably belongs in other sections and some Things are probably left out. I hope it will serve as a basis for discussion.
  We still need to say who we are & what audience we are addressing.
  Good luck @ The meeting. Sorry I'm missing it (but not very)!

Love, Jul

Wallah!!

Y ALLRIGHT!!!!!!!  here it is!!!!!!!!!!!

(Damn typewriter!  Even the celebrationary hoot is screwed up!)  Working on

the editing was most therapeutic — kept me from really crashing out here.  Wish

I could be there for the layout too (I'd hoped to hitch a ride out with the guy

next door whose wife is now in Madison — but she's coming HERE in Feb instead  ☹ )

I am most excited to think it may soon be over (I know, I sound like all the

hostage announcements? —)  Anyhow, if there's any additional work to do, I

(unfortunately) xxx have the time to do it.

                                                           from Barb

Hope all is going well with all of you.  I miss you all terribly.

# Chapter 8

# Communication Skills

Communication skills are vital in any group that uses consensus decision making. To use consensus, participants must not only be able to impart information effectively, but must also be able to understand each other when their opinions, values, or feelings differ. Communication skills are necessary for meetings to work well and for facilitation to be effective. These skills are also important during the day-to-day operation of the group, as members develop the relationships that help them use consensus at meetings. *(See Chapter 11, TECHNIQUES FOR GROUP BUILDING, for more about the importance of communication in this respect, and for some sample communication exercises.)*

The goal of communication is to increase understanding between people for a variety of purposes. You may want to exchange information needed for a decision, express feelings so others will know why an issue is important to you, ask for something you need, or increase understanding for its own sake--because it feels good. In this chapter we present some techniques that can make communication more effective. Many of the skills we describe are actually tools for preventing or clearing up misunderstanding. Since misunderstanding is most troublesome when it involves feelings or criticism, we will emphasize these personal

areas. But we want to stress that the principles and skills described here are useful in all kinds of communication, including group discussions where ideas and opinions are exchanged.

## LISTENING

Communication involves more than just accurately transmitting information: it also requires that people know they are being understood. Speakers need responses that let them know the other person hears and cares about what they are expressing. They also need to know what the listener thinks or feels in response. Good communication is a cooperative activity in which people share responsibility, help and support each other. (Sounds like consensus decision making, doesn't it? It is.)

### Listen Actively

People tend to think of the listener's role as a passive one. The listener receives from and is acted upon by the speaker. A good listener, though, shares the responsibility for increasing understanding by paying close attention and trying to understand. Good listening means using your own communication skills to help the speaker get the message across.

There are several specific things you can do as a listener:

--<u>Make an effort to really hear</u> what the speaker is saying. Try to put yourself in the speaker's shoes and see things from her or his perspective. Refrain from making any judgments for the time being. Withholding judgment will help you be more open to what is said and will help create a non-threatening climate in which feelings, beliefs and values can be expressed.

--<u>Let the speaker know</u> that you are listening, that you care. All those little signals (eye contact, head nods, "Yeah, I know") can reassure the speaker that you are involved and that you are making an effort to understand.

--When you don't understand, <u>seek more information</u>. Ask questions or paraphrase. (The use of questions and paraphrasing is discussed below.)

## Examine Your Assumptions

People make generalizations all the time--there is no avoiding it. They take specific bits of information and draw conclusions from them. (Barb is reading *The Women's Room*, so Barb must be a feminist.) This kind of logical reasoning is the way the human mind works. But in a quest for understanding, assumptions about other people, or what they mean, may be wrong, or incomplete, or may close your mind to the true significance of new information from that person. To reduce the misunderstanding that assumptions can cause, try to be aware of the conclusions you draw about others. Be conscious that they are just speculation. Think about what information has led you to make those assumptions and recognize that there are other conclusions you might make from that same information. When an assumption about another person affects the way you communicate with her or him, you might want to share the assumption with the person and find out if it is valid, explaining why you are doing so.

*Try to put yourself in the speaker's shoe and see things from her or his perspective*

Example: You might say, "Last week when I asked you about your medical problems, you didn't want to talk about them. So I'm assuming you would rather I didn't ever bring up that subject. Am I right?"

By explaining why you have made particular assumptions, you offer others the opportunity to give you new information or explanations. At the same time, you increase their understanding by letting them know what you think and why.

## Paraphrase

Paraphrasing is a useful tool for clarifying communication during a conversation. It allows the speaker to know how well she or he is being understood and provides a second chance if a message was misperceived the first time. Paraphrasing consists of summarizing or restating what you have heard, in your own words, and asking the speaker if that is what was really meant.

Example: In response to repeated complaints on the theme of "I'm sick of all this extra work," you might say, "I think what I hear you saying is that you have had to pick up a lot more work since John left, and you don't think that's fair. You want the rest of the staff to pitch in more. Is that what you mean?"

A tool related to paraphrasing is expressing the unstated message you think you hear "between the lines" and seeing whether your perceptions are accurate. ("I get the impression that you would like me to offer to take over one of your projects. Is that what you want?") It's important not to do this kind of "reading between the lines" in an accusing way. Use this tentative paraphrasing gently and sensitively.

This technique is tricky. Often mis-used. Sometimes an easy defense. Maybe cite The source? (To Carl Rogers. Its his "client-centered response".) Gotta be tuned in to The speaker emotionally for This to work.
from Michael

Got this as an artifact

## Ask Supportive Questions

Questions are an obvious technique for getting information needed to understand the speaker's message better. Often it is up to the listener to ask questions because the speaker does not know what

parts of the message are unclear, or that she or he has wrongly assumed a common background of information, a shared interpretation, or an insight that the listener does not have.

Questions can also be supportive. They tell the speaker that you are interested and care about understanding. Sometimes asking questions lets the speaker know that it's OK with you to discuss a subject that she or he finds difficult to talk about. On the other hand, sometimes questions can put pressure on a speaker and make her or him feel challenged or "on the spot." A person can be embarrassed by a question she or he cannot or doesn't want to answer. So be sensitive to the effects of your questions. A period of silence after a question may signal discomfort, or it may mean that the speaker is taking a question seriously and is thinking about the answer. Don't assume too quickly that it means one or the other. Do, however, be willing to withdraw a question if it is causing the speaker unnecessary discomfort.

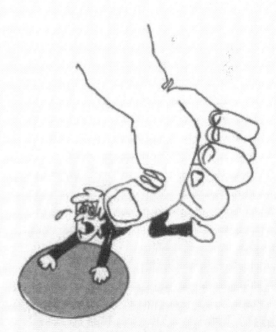

*Sometimes questions can put pressure on a speaker and make her or him feel "on the spot."*

**63**

There are two basic kinds of questions. An open-ended question allows an unlimited choice of responses. A closed-ended question has only two, or a small number, of possible responses. "How are you feeling right now?" is open ended. "Are you mad at me?" is closed, since the only possible answers are "yes" and "no." Usually open-ended questions are preferable since they don't lead the speaker, but allow her or him to respond in the way she or he wants. Use closed-ended questions when you need specific, defined information. Another tip is that positively phrased questions are usually more supportive than negative ones. "How could we have managed this meeting better?" is more hopeful, encouraging, and perhaps more productive than "What did we do wrong?"

## Levels of Responses

Most of the things people say can be taken on three levels:

--Content: The facts or information of the message.

--Sentiment: How the speaker feels about what she or he is saying.

--Intent: The reason for making the statement.

You can respond to another person's statement on any one of these levels. For example, Jane might say, "I sent my article about our new energy saving system to the community newspaper. Do you think they'll print it?" A content response to the question might be, "Well, I know they only print about half the articles they receive, but it's been awhile since they had anything on that topic, so the chances are better than 50-50." A response at the level of sentiment might be, "Don't be nervous. I think you did a great job and if they don't print it, it won't be your fault." An intent response is one that considers the question, "Why did Jane say what she just said to me?" In this case, such a response might be, "Are you asking my opinion because of my own newspaper ex-

perience? I'd be glad to review the article and give you my opinion, if that's what you want."

Since each of these responses is potentially an accurate reply to the message, it can be hard to know when a response is "off," not at the speaker's intended level. Sometimes even the speaker cannot identify why she or he feels a vague discomfort about a conversation, thinking, "We are talking about the subject I brought up. Why am I not getting what I want out of the conversation?"

Example: Al might say, "My truck needs new tires," and Liz might respond on the sentiment level, "Gee, you must be frustrated. Everything goes wrong with your truck, and now this. I know how you must feel." Chances are that Al might continue speaking on Liz's level. "Yes, I'm sick and tired of dealing with that old truck." Or, "No, I'm not upset. I've known the tires were wearing out for a long time and I've been saving for new ones." It is easy for Al to accept Liz's response at face value because it is accurate or reasonable, without realizing that he is uncomfortable with the conversation because he'd hoped to communicate on the content level. Liz might have said, "I know something about tires. What brand are you planning to buy?" and Al would have been satisfied by an accurate response at his intended level.

Different people are more comfortable communicating at different levels and may automatically reply at the same level most of the time. Try to be alert to all three levels and develop your ability to respond at each of them. When something about a conversation seems "off," use your awareness of the different levels to diagnose if responding at the wrong level is the problem. If you have doubts, ask about the other person's intent.

**64**

Example: "Are you telling me about all your bad experiences because you want emotional support? Or were you telling me your problems so I won't repeat your mistakes? Or is it some other reason?"

## FEEDBACK AND CRITICISM

Feedback and criticism are potentially frightening activities. Sometimes it is very threatening to hear what another person thinks about you. It is equally risky to talk to someone about observations or problems you have with them. Yet often when people avoid giving feedback or criticism for too long, the situation gets worse and worse, or the feelings become increasingly intense, and an originally minor problem becomes a major crisis. It is easier to give needed feedback and criticism if you know specific communication techniques that promote clear communication and minimize threat. The techniques described below work best when they are used in a supportive atmosphere among people who trust each other. Some people find it easier to give and receive criticism in a group, when they are surrounded by friends who provide emotional support, and who can add their own insights or perceptions to the discussion. Others prefer the privacy of one-on-one interaction where they can focus exclusively on the person they are talking to, and where they feel less vulnerable.

## Feedback

Feedback is telling another person how you perceive what she or he did or said. Usually your perceptions are closely tied to some kind of judgment you have made about that behavior, an interpretation or evaluation. When you give feedback to someone, it is important to separate the specific behavior from your judgment about it. If you tell Bill he is lazy, he will probably not know why you think that. If you specify that he is behind on his work load, or that he doesn't put the lids back on jars, he will know what you are talking about. (And what is going to be more productive to talk about? An abstract concept like laziness, or specific behaviors like keeping up with a work load?) The most useful feedback describes rather than evaluates. It is specific rather than general. And if it does include some kind of interpretation on your part, it should be stated in tentative rather than absolute terms. ("You seem like you have a lot of enthusiasm for this project," rather than, "You're really in a hurry to dive into this.")

## Criticism

Criticism is a complex process that includes feedback. Criticism is appropriate when another person's behavior, as you have observed it, has caused a problem and when you are dissatisfied and want change. The process of criticism includes telling the other person your observations, explaining how you feel about their behaviors, and stating what you want to be different and why.

RE: Communication Skills section and scope:
    The sections on Commun. skills, emotions, etc. are good, but they stray far from consensus per se. There's too much here, says Joe; it strays too far from what he'd expect a consensus manual to include; He suggests cutting back on the commun. section, editing back to the skills directly related to facilitating the reaching of consensus, for instance, talking about eye contact as an important tool for the facilitator to use in assessing if someone is finished speaking, or wants to speak, etc.
    Joe is also making an aesthetic judgment about the scope of the book as it now stands. He thinks it lacks unity, is kind of unweildy. He suggests using Appendices for the less-central material.

Although it often has negative connotations in this culture, criticism can be used in a positive, growth-oriented way. It can help groups to see new and better ways of working together. A constructively critical process can enhance group unity by correcting misunderstandings and relieving fears that keep group members from working together effectively. These positive effects are most likely to happen when criticism is separated from blame and approached as a shared, cooperative process.

Before you criticize someone, ask yourself:

--Is it an appropriate time to discuss this topic?

--Is the person in a good emotional state to receive criticism?

--Am I in a good frame of mind myself? (Or do I just want to strike out somewhere because of other frustrations I am feeling?)

--Is the behavior or problem something that the other person has the power to change?

--Am I willing to take responsibility for helping to make that change? (This might include being specific about what you want, maintaining the relationship long enough to provide necessary emotional support, being open to compromise or change yourself.)

--Has the person indicated a willingness to hear the criticism? Is it about something she or he has been told before and chosen not to act on?

Steps for giving criticism:

1. If the criticism is potentially upsetting for the other person, or if it will require a long discussion, then ask first whether this is a good time for the person to talk about something important.

2. Begin by giving feedback about the specific behavior you are responding to. Behavioral feedback requires a description of what was done and includes statements prefaced with, "When I saw you do . . ." -- "You said a few minutes ago that . . ." It is an observation without evaluating what you saw.

3. The next step is to identify how you feel about the behavior. Verbalizing feelings independently of the stated observation has several advantages: a) it reduces the chance that the criticism will be misinterpreted; b) it allows others to understand your feelings and to correct you if they think your interpretation is wrong; and c) it expresses mutual responsibility by assuming that your feelings and the other person's behavior combine to make a shared problem.

66

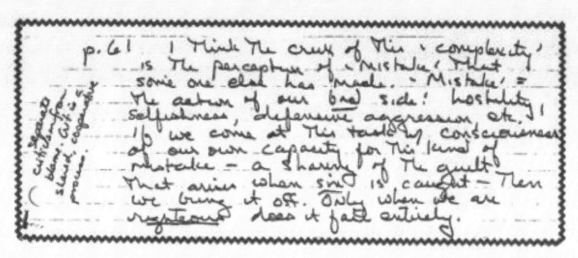

p. 61  I think the crux of this 'complexity' is the perception of a 'mistake' that someone else has made. 'Mistake' = the action of our bad side! hostility, selfishness, defensive aggression etc. If we come at this task by consciousness of our own capacity for this kind of mistake — a sharing of the guilt that arises when sin is caught — then we bring it off. Only when we are righteous does it fail entirely.

Example: A feeling statement after a description of the behavior might be, "When you take time off to chat with your friends during working hours, I have to cover for you and then I think I am being taken advantage of and I get angry."

4. You also have to <u>state what you want the other person to do differently</u>. Make clear what you want them to <u>do</u> (not feel, think or be). Say what you want, not what you don't want. ("I want you to tell me when you think I am being rude to you," rather than, "I don't want you to hide your feelings from me.")

If there is any question about who you are addressing, make that clear. If you say to a group, "Some of us need to be more careful about cleaning up after ourselves," everyone will wonder who you mean, and if it could be themselves. ("I think I left a dirty coffee cup out last week. I wonder if he's mad at me.") It's better to be direct about who you are talking to.

5. The final step is to <u>say why you want the change</u>. Explaining "why" might require a statement about your own values ("I really like to work in a clean office") or it may clarify how the change in behavior will help you ("If I'm not distracted, I can get my work done more quickly"). Openly expressing your own values and needs helps to make criticism a cooperative process. The other person can better understand the reasons for

your criticism and has an opportunity to object if your reasons seem wrong or unfair. Sharing information also increases the likelihood of a mutually agreeable change.

<u>Receiving criticism</u>: When you are being criticized, try to listen well, using the techniques described above under "Listening." The following rules are helpful to remember.

1. <u>Listen carefully</u> to what the person is saying. Refrain initially from expressing your agreement or disagreement. Simply show that you have understood. Paraphrasing is helpful here. You might say, "The problem, then, as you see it, is . . . ." -- "If I understand you correctly, you feel we should . . . ." After you have summarized what you heard, give the person a chance to agree or disagree with your perceptions. Continue to listen actively and paraphrase until all misunderstanding seems to be resolved and you believe that you understand what the person thinks, feels, and would like to see happen to change things.

2. <u>Wait quietly through pauses</u> in the conversation to encourage the other person to say all that may be on her or his mind. Don't rush to fill silences.

3. <u>Use open-ended questions</u> to encourage the person to continue talking. "How did you feel about that?" -- "Is there anything else that's bothering you?" -- "Where do you think we disagree?"

**67**

4. Don't take the focus of the conversation away from the person who is criticizing you by disagreeing or by talking about yourself, your thoughts, or your perceptions. Delay your response until you have heard what she or he has to say and you have used paraphrasing or other techniques to check your understanding of the criticism. Only when you understand, and the other person agrees that you understand, is it time to respond with your own perceptions and feelings.

## CONCLUSION

The techniques described above are tools for communicating more effectively. If used judiciously, you can communicate better yourself and can help others to do so as well. Please do not treat these tools as dogma or use them to gain an unfair advantage over people who have not learned the skills. An unsympathetic use of verbal proficiency by one person can intimidate others who are less skilled, and can cause resentment. Communication in consensus groups should be used to increase understanding among people, and the tools described in this chapter should be used toward that end.

MOST HIGHLY RECOMMENDED RESOURCES

*PARENT EFFECTIVENESS TRAINING* by Thomas Gordon

*JOINING TOGETHER* by Frank and David Johnson

*CONSTRUCTIVE CRITICISM* by Gracie Lyons

*"Face Saving, Criticism and Defensiveness"* by Celeste Rice

"Astronomically, it's spring. Meteorologically, it is NOT spring." – Brian
Spring, 1979

From Jan, 1979
Fall, 1979, Thursday –

Well – late as ever here it comes. C'est la vie. I still had a good time writing it with Crepps – He wrote parts of it. I think this is a section that we may want to elaborate on a lot more. I'm not sure what it should be called. "Prefer" doesn't quite give me what I'm looking for and "Who we are" is incomplete.

# Working With Emotions

## WHY BE CONCERNED ABOUT FEELINGS?

Attention to emotions in a group is a practical and sometimes a necessary part of getting the group's work done.

--A constructive and sensitive look at members' feelings may not only point out problems that might otherwise be overlooked, but can also be the spark of energy by which creative solutions are found.

--Working directly with feelings can avert serious problems those feelings could cause if left unattended. A "hidden agenda," for example, is an unexpressed motivation that leads a group member to behave a certain way, or to promote a certain decision.

> Example: Dan may urge the group to act quickly on a certain proposal for a number of reasons which he explains to the group. But his hidden agenda may be the fact that he is in a bad mood and wants the meeting to end quickly so he can go home.

A group can work together better when members try to be aware of their hidden agendas and address them when they cause problems.

--At times the whole group will experience feelings that disrupt their work. In such cases, it's better to respond to those feelings and do something about them than to limp along with an ineffective process.

--You may want to try to affect the emotional climate in a way that will help the group, to increase members' happiness and satisfaction so they will continue to be active members. To do this, you must address members' feelings and the things that affect those feelings.

Feelings are an important part of the experience of working with a group. Most people value being in a group for emotional reasons: it feels good to be with people they like, to share with others, and to get emotional support for the work they are doing. But since feelings can be hard to understand, to control, or to predict, groups often ignore their emotional experience and focus on the "thinking work" at hand. Since most people aren't as skilled or confident in working with emotions as they are at functioning rationally, they often just hope that the feelings will take care of themselves.

Most of the time you can get away with neglecting emotions because the norm in this culture is not to show strong feelings except to a few, intimate friends. Yet those emotions are there and they affect the group and its individual members. People may be experiencing any of a wide range of pleasant or unpleasant feelings or attitudes toward other group members, toward the whole group, or toward the world at large. These feelings are an important part of the group's experience and members need to be able to respond to those feelings when it becomes necessary.

## THE SOURCES OF FEELINGS IN GROUPS

Sometimes it doesn't matter where feelings come from--the important question is what to do about them. At times, though, identifying the source of certain emotions can help you handle their effects. Below are some places to look for sources of feelings.

One obvious source of feelings is the immediate situation in the group. For instance, you may feel a sense of urgency that a proposed measure be adopted; you may feel angry or hurt about a comment that ignores or belittles your perspective; you may feel pleased about how well your group works together and feel a secure, happy sense of belonging. These kinds of feelings arise from a specific, immediate situation.

Another source of feelings in a group is past interactions. You may hold a grudge from a time in the past when you didn't get what you thought you should. Resentments remaining from past struggles over power issues might bring anger, guilt, fear, and other feelings into play. Whatever their source, emotions rooted in past experiences are usually less clear and understandable than feelings arising from current events.

A third source of feelings is a group's natural emotional cycles. There are two types of cycles. The first, the work-emotion cycle, involves the feelings that arise out of the group's normal work process. For example, working in a meeting is often frustrating. The frustration builds up until the group needs to blow off steam by joking, arguing, gossiping, stretching, generally relaxing and refocusing. This type of cycle is natural and should be expected. *(See the "Meeting Phases" section of Chapter 6, STRUCTURING YOUR MEETINGS.)*

A group's emotional life cycle also affects members' feelings. There are certain points in a group's history when members have more specific emotional needs than at other times: when the group is first forming, when it adds new members, when it changes its goals and direction, when individuals in the group give up something familiar, such as an accustomed role or control over a task they've handled for awhile. These times are emotionally difficult because members are uncertain of how to act in the group and because they are re-negotiating power and influence relations in the group. Such periods are often marked with open conflict; almost always members will feel some tension.

**70**

## DIAGNOSIS: WHAT'S GOING ON?

While you're thinking about the sources of feelings in a group, look to your intuitions. Often you'll know that emotions are affecting group process, without being sure what the feelings are or how they're working. If you sense that the feelings are important, don't be afraid to ask the affected members what's going on.

It's useful to remember that this culture generally discourages people from expressing feelings, so even a wrought-up group may not be showing much emotion outwardly. A group that has not built up a base of mutual trust will be less open in showing feelings than will a relaxed and trusting group. An individual who doesn't yet trust the group also tends to be less open. As you look at the group, keep in mind the degree of trust and openness, and be sensitive to subtle expression (or suppression) of emotions.

Tension and boredom in a group may be signs that emotions are influencing the group's process or progress. Some indications of tension are: long uncomfortable silences (as opposed to comfortable periods of quiet), lack of eye contact, people withdrawing into themselves, outbursts of anger, one person dominating the discussion while others hold back, a general lack of sharpness or focus in the group, noticeably more or less joking and noisiness or quietness than usual, or people talking more quietly or loudly than usual. Common signs of boredom include wandering eyes, coughing, slow responses to questions, and of course, snoring.

Remember, though, that all these behaviors are also ordinary and normal to some degree. Please do not over-analyze your group. No group is always smooth and ideally "together." In fact, groups often _value_ tension as a prerequisite to creativity, and awkwardness as a sign of humanness. Look for these signs only in conjunction with your own intuitive sense about feelings in your group. They may help you see concretely what you only vaguely sensed before.

## WHEN FEELINGS ARE A PROBLEM

There are two kinds of strategies you can follow when you see feelings are having an undesirable effect on a group. You can either do nothing, or you can intervene—take action to change the situation.

The first option, non-intervention, is often ignored. People usually try to smooth away anger, hurt feelings or sorrow because they fear such unpleasant emotions. Rarely do members take advantage of the constructive role that emotional struggles can play in moving a group along to creative changes and growth. Even if the feelings are not likely to have a long-range positive effect, it still may do more harm than good to bring the emotional state of the group out into the open. The feelings may be caused by something you have no power to change (a crisis in the private life of a group member, the candidate you worked so hard for lost the election) and talking about it right now might just make people feel worse. Perhaps it's just one of those things that will blow over. Perhaps it's something that needs to be dealt with, but this isn't the right time. Keep in mind that often the best action is nothing other than flowing with the current of events.

If you decide to intervene, there are two ways of doing so: you can diagnose the need and try to fill it without talking about it; or you can talk with the group about what you see, and suggest action or get the group to decide what to do.

As an example of the former case, you might notice that the group is restless and suggest a break. You don't have to tell the group that it is restless. Your intervention can move the group to a state where it can get work done, but it doesn't require that everyone re-direct their attention to the group's process. It is especially helpful if many members

of the group are alert to signs of feelings in the group and can share the role of intervening or facilitating on the emotional level.

The other option is to openly intervene by telling the group what feelings you sense. The group as a whole may then choose to discuss the feelings and act on them. This is the most straightforward approach, and working together on feelings can strengthen and unify a group. Some potential problems with this approach are that it can increase tension in the group and distract it from the task at hand. If the group fails to respond well, the effect can be demoralizing.

Most groups find some kind of balance between the amount of energy they put

## AN "OPEN" INTERVENTION

A group of demonstrators had been blockading a nuclear power plant. Unexpectedly, a large number of guards rushed from inside the plant grounds, picked the demonstrators up bodily, and hurled them aside in order to allow a new shift of workers to be rushed through the gate. The demonstrators, physically and psychically bruised, met to decide what to do next. Frustration and anger were causing much tension, and people were close to flying off the handle. They were not thinking clearly and were more concerned about revenge than about the original purpose of the demonstration. Finally, one man said, "I don't like the way we are feeling and acting right now. Can we sing a song to calm ourselves down?" The group spent about five minutes singing a peaceful song. People relaxed, began thinking clearly again, and were able to get a better perspective on the situation. They went home feeling good about themselves and each other, ready to plan for the next step in a long campaign. A violent reaction was averted and positive energy was re-ignited for working towards the group's goals.

## A "SILENT" INTERVENTION

CCR met to have a potluck in one member's home. It was intended to precede another long, difficult meeting in a series of tense meetings with overloaded agendas. One member came to the meeting grieving over a personal tragedy that had occurred recently, and he described his feelings to the group during the check-in time that normally begins our meetings. Other members, feeling this person's sadness, and also knowing that the group as a whole needed to nourish each other more than we needed to address our work for the night, dropped the meeting's agenda in an unspoken agreement. The evening was spent sitting quietly around the table, reminiscing about memories, and learning about each other's past experiences. Sharing these things quietly with each other allowed us to go home feeling re-connected as a group. We got a little further behind on our tasks, but in the long run group unity and commitment towards those tasks was improved. The meeting is still remembered as a special time that reminded each of us why we have chosen to work together.

into working on feelings and the amount they focus on their tasks. Too much time spent on feelings can be exhausting and can keep the group from getting work done. Too little time on feelings may result in members feeling unsupported and becoming alienated, or may hurt group cohesion because members don't have a chance to feel personally involved with each other.

When you are deciding what approach to use for responding to emotions in your group, consider the group, the problem or situation, what your goals are, and what you yourself are comfortable with.

## Specific Intervention Techniques for Responding to Feelings

If you opt for some kind of intervention, there are several techniques you can use. Some are better suited to working with "positive" feelings and some are better for "negative" ones. Some are applicable to both kinds of situations.

--Energy and excitement can be channeled productively into a brainstorming session that will bring out lots of good ideas. Round robin excitement sharing can bring out the good feelings more explicitly. Or the group can applaud or celebrate itself in some other way, such as a dance or song.

--A session spent working with anger, fear, or other unpleasant feelings can start with a minute of silence. Each person can use this time to identify and clarify his or her own feelings, and to become composed enough to prevent a destructive interchange later on. Silence is an opportunity for members to think for a moment without distraction, but it has benefits that go beyond the rational thought that occurs during this period. Silence is often soothing, allows members to become "centered," and breaks the flow of competitive, overexcited interchange. Often during silence, a member will realize that a point he or she was arguing for so urgently isn't really that important after all.

--"Fears in the hat" is a useful device for dealing with people's worries and developing empathy and solidarity in the group. Have each person write down a fear they have about a problem (or another feeling about a stated topic). Put the unsigned slips of paper into a hat. Then pass the hat around and have each person draw a paper, read it, and say how he or she feels about it. Can he or she empathize, give encouragement, or identify with the feelings expressed? This exercise can help members see the common lines of feelings in the group. They may feel relieved to hear their own fears stated by others, or they might get a new perspective on what others are feeling.

**73**

--"Light and Livelies," or quick games, help people loosen up and feel like full human beings rather than thinking machines. These activities may also lessen or smooth out bad feelings that arose in recent discussion. Of course, games also take advantage of the good energy in a group. *(For a fuller explanation of this technique, see the section entitled "Encourage Social Interaction" in Chapter 11, TECHNIQUES FOR GROUP BUILDING.)*

--Finally, at times, emotions are best dealt with in an informal way, outside the group meeting. The facilitator or another member might take responsibility for checking on someone's feelings during a break or after the meeting. Or if there is a conflict between two people the disputants may decide to deal with it later, between themselves.

## Long-Range Techniques for Your Group

There will always be occasional little emotional crises that pop up from time to time and need to be dealt with on the spot, using techniques like the ones described above. A lot can be done, though, to build your group's ability to deal with day-to-day feelings an a healthy way. Below are some suggestions.

--Try to foster in your group a habit of communicating openly about feelings. You, as an individual, can help this along by acting as a model, expressing your own feelings, and encouraging others to do so by asking supportive questions.

--End all meetings with an evaluation session. By promoting opportunities for members to speak personally, be open with their feelings, and be specific in their comments, your group can avoid defensiveness and build trust in its members. *(See "Evaluations" in Chapter 6, STRUCTURING YOUR MEETINGS.)*

--Hold occasional meetings for the purpose of dealing with feelings. Members can be encouraged to talk about their feelings about the group, about others in the group, about their own role, or other pertinent issues. These sessions can take the form of a weekend retreat, a twice-a-year general evaluation session, or whatever seems best for the group.

*See Chapter 11, TECHNIQUES FOR GROUP BUILDING, for more ideas about how to develop a group that can deal with feelings in a constructive and supportive way.*

## Talking About Fears and Resentments

Outbursts of anger or disgust often signal an opening up, like a dam bursting. Your first tendency might be to try to cool things down, but sometimes it's a good idea to take advantage of this expression of previously-suppressed feelings. The problem is that while the outburst of hard feelings can be a catalyst for constructive change and movement, many people have trouble talking about the fears and anger which they may have towards other group members. Because they want to avoid conflict, because they don't want to hurt others or make them angry, because they are afraid of being wrong, or because they just don't have a good opportunity, members often hold these feelings inside. This

can allow tensions to build up and misunderstandings to occur, thus interfering
with participants' enjoyment of the
group's work.

Groups that practice radical therapy use
a specific technique to get these feelings out in the open.  They plan a certain time in a meeting when members can
express "paranoid fantasies" and "held
resentments."

A "paranoid fantasy" is a fear about
someone else's thoughts, feelings or
intentions.  This is Ron's chance to say,
"Dina, you kept looking out the window
while I was talking a while ago, and I
was afraid you were disapproving of my
ideas, but didn't want to say so."  Since
a fear of this kind is always based on
some kind of experience, Dina should
answer Ron by searching for whatever
grain of truth she can find in his fear
and responding to it.  Perhaps he was
right; if so, Dina should acknowledge
it.  Perhaps Dina didn't disapprove of
Ron's ideas, but her mind was wandering
to some personal concerns and it was
understandable that Ron should take her
inattention personally.  In that case,
she should explain.

"Held resentments" are private angers or
irritations with the behavior of others
in the group.  Perhaps these angers seem
petty, or unjustified, or perhaps they
signify a greater underlying conflict.
Whatever the case, the feelings are real.
Expressing them in an honest, respectful
way to the person involved brings the
problems out in the light where they can
be taken care of, or simply acknowledged.
*(A good way of expressing "held resent-
ments" is described under "Feedback and
Criticism" in Chapter 8, COMMUNICATION
SKILLS.)*

You may not want to set aside time for
these feelings at all your meetings, but
it is useful to do so occasionally.
Besides giving group members an opportunity to express hidden feelings, it
will give them a chance to learn how to
work with the feelings.  It also helps

the group acknowledge the importance of
paying attention to feelings, which may
encourage members to express fears and
angers more constructively at all times.

## WHEN FEELINGS HELP A GROUP

We want to remind you that all those
good-feeling emotions are important and
require attention, too!  Shared excitement, love for each other, satisfaction
with the group's work, and good humor
are all part of the rewards of being in
a good group.  These feelings should be
valued and nurtured.  The group may want
to analyze:  "Where does this feeling
come from?  What can we do to make it
happen in the future?"  The suggestions
above for analyzing the sources of feelings and responding to them are applicable here.

Occasionally, exuberant high spirits
will get in the way of doing an important task.  In such an instance, you
may choose to give in to those feelings,
deciding that the good group experience
is worth a loss of time at work.  If the
work has to be done, though, you can
intervene by using a group activity that
burns excess energy and allows expression of all those happy feelings that
are trying to burst out--perhaps a group
song--before digging back into work.

75

Sometimes unpleasant emotions are good for the group, too, and should be temporarily encouraged. Open expression of conflict can clear the air and make the group aware of problems that need to be solved. At times anger at social wrongs is valuable because it gives people energy to work for change. A strong expression of anger or pain by one group member can make everyone aware of how important it is to change a bad situation.

> STay away from use of word "position" — implies Territory which has to be defended.

Claire —

Here we are! I was up all night last night - finished @ 5:30 this a.m. (Feels so good to meet a deadline, for once.)

I had 25 copies run off. You can get more than these. But lets try to just give them to people who will *really* give us feedback. (the printing was about $75!)

Redundancy still rides the waves — in ways I hadn't realyzed.

I'm uncomfortable about how many examples are from my experience, or mention CCR. Need stuff from other people — & some stuff that mentions ICC's experience.

But I feel really good. We have a ways to go from here, but I'm excited about it.

Good luck if the New School.

Jim!

# Chapter 10

# Conflict and Problem Solving

Conflict is a natural, healthy part of
any group's process. In fact, if there
is little or no conflict in your group,
you should be suspicious. Members may
be holding back some of their real
thoughts and feelings because they are
afraid that expressing disagreement
might be destructive to the group or
the people in it. This is dangerous.
Conflict that is suppressed and stored
up can lead to smoldering resentments
that might erupt in the future. It's
true that conflict can be destructive.
If the group handles it properly, however, conflict can also be constructive,
leading to greater clarity, creativity
and growth.

### GUIDELINES FOR RESPONDING TO CONFLICT

If you have been reading this handbook
straight through up to this point, most
of the concepts described below will already be familiar to you. The same
group skills and principles that are
useful in consensus decision making are
also useful for responding to conflict.
You might want to treat this chapter as
a quick review of some of the most important points expressed earlier, as
well as a good framework to fall back
on when there is a conflict in your
group and you need to know what to do.

1. Accept conflict as natural. Don't
be afraid of it. When conflict occurs in
your group, treat it as an opportunity to
examine the issues involved in depth and
to learn more about the underlying values
and assumptions you hold. Accept the
challenge to find imaginative and creative responses to conflicting ideas.

2. Bring hidden conflicts out in the
open. If you think there is a conflict
hidden under the surface that is causing
problems in the group, call it out at an
appropriate time. If you see signs of
unexpressed disagreement, ask those involved what they are feeling.

3.  Disagree with ideas, not with people.  Don't accuse or blame group members who are in conflict with you.  Try to put yourself in their shoes: what are their needs, values, assumptions and previous experiences?  Remember that your goal is to work together to find a mutually acceptable solution.  This task may be difficult when you're in the heat of an argument, but do it to the degree that you can.  No matter how intense a conflict is, never turn a disagreement over ideas, beliefs, procedures or plans into a personal attack against another person.

4.  When defining an issue or problem, always define it as shared.  Responsibility for a conflict never lies with just one person or faction.  Say, "We do not agree about distribution of office space," not "Jack refuses to share his desk."  Say, "Mary and Tom have a problem coordinating their work schedules," not "Tom is never around when Mary needs to consult with him."

5.  Identify and focus on the most important, central issues to the conflict.  Sometimes a group will flounder in general disagreement or confusion about a decision until someone "sharpens" the conflict by pointing out where the most basic point of contention seems to be.  Focusing on this issue may have the short-range effect of escalating conflict, but it is a necessary step to understanding and dealing with disagreement.

Example:  Your group is trying to decide whether to donate some money to the strike fund of a local union that needs support.  The discussion touches on political issues, how long the strike is likely to last, how much the group can afford, expected expenses coming up, how responsible your group is to contributors who have given it money to spend on its own projects.  Then someone says, "It seems to me that the real issue here is whether or not we need to keep some money in reserve for emergencies.  I think Susan and Rich are saying that it's important to do that, while Pat

is saying that we need to use our funds, not hoard them up."  This statement turns out to be right on target and leads to a heated debate.  But now the group is focused on working out the central issue, rather than discussing peripheral topics on which there is little basic disagreement.

To identify what is the central issue for you, don't argue just for the sake of arguing.  Instead of dwelling on what is wrong with a statement you disagree with, try looking for what is right.  There may be areas where you just can't find rightness, ideas which you cannot bring yourself to accept:  these are the important issues in the conflict.  Your reasons may be based in logical principles, or they may have to do with feelings.  Both are legitimate.  Once you feel you understand the important issues in a conflict, don't get sidetracked into tangential subjects.

6.  Don't polarize the conflicting positions.  It is easy to start looking at a conflict in terms of mutually exclusive positions.  ("You are either with me or against me.")  This attitude may blind participants to the wide range of directions, viewpoints, and decisions that will be available if they keep their minds open.

7.  Don't compromise too quickly.  By "compromise," we mean a solution that is halfway between the opposing viewpoints, in which each side gets part, but not all of what it wanted.  Compromise often seems to be the fairest response, or at least an easy way to end a conflict quickly.  And sometimes after considering a problem in depth, a group may decide that a compromise is a necessary, or even the best solution.  By compromising too quickly, however, you may not adequately explore the problem and its potential solutions.  The ideal solution to a conflict is a creative one which finds a way to give everyone what they most need.

Example: A few members of a collective store argue that the store should be open on Saturdays. Many of the clientele they are trying to serve do their shopping on Saturday, and frequently express disappointment that the store isn't open then. Other staff members are against this proposal because they value having the whole weekend free. An obvious compromise would be to have the store open on alternate Saturdays, or to have it open Saturday mornings only As the argument progresses, however, a solution is found that answers both sides' needs. The store will be open every Saturday, and the collective will hire someone part-time from the community to staff the store on those days. Anticipated increased business on Saturdays will provide the revenue to pay the additional salary.

8. If you aren't centrally involved in a conflict, don't take sides too quickly. The guidelines described above are often difficult to follow for persons who are emotionally embroiled in a heated debate. By remaining nonpartisan, you can better watch the process of the meeting and help see that the guidelines are being followed. This doesn't mean that you shouldn't develop and express your opinion--you should. But at the same time, try to keep an open mind. If you delay committing yourself to a particular position, you will be able to consider more information that comes out in later discussion, and you will have more time to think about the issue.

9. Try to be aware of your own feelings and opinions during a conflict. The more you can clearly express what is most important to you, what you really need and want, the better you will be able to communicate and negotiate with others. Very often people get sidetracked into intellectual, practical, or political discussions because they are not aware of, or don't express, what they really feel.

Example: Jan, Celeste and Chel were planning a workshop agenda. A particular activity had been suggested and Chel kept coming up with practical reasons why the activity wouldn't work. Jan and Celeste kept responding to Chel's statements by telling her why the activity would work. Finally Chel said, "Wait a minute. I'm just thinking of all these problems because I really hate that activity and I don't want to do it. In this case, Jan and Celeste said, "OK. Then let's try to think of a different activity." They _might_ have said, "Can we go ahead and do the activity, but you find a role for yourself that you wouldn't mind too much?" or "We understand your feelings, but we would like to go ahead and do the activity. Will you agree to it, even though you don't like it?" or "Let's talk about your feelings about the activity and see if we can identify why you don't like it and what we can do about it." All of these responses deal with the real problem, once it has been identified. But until Chel stated her true feelings, the group was bogged down in a pointless discussion of imaginary problems.

You can also help other group members identify their feelings if they are not doing so themselves. In the example above, Jan or Celeste might have said to Chel, "It seems that you don't want to do this activity. Is there some reason why, other than the ones you are saying?" People tend to think that their needs and wants should be logically justifi-

LANGUAGE:
    Ailsa says: I don't like calling any feelings "negative."

    Joe says: "Objections" is the language of Parliamentary Procedure.
Revise out, substitute with "concerns" or "resentments" or etc.

able, so they often resort to rational arguments about subjects that actually have to do with their feelings. It is legitimate, however, to say, "I feel uncomfortable about this, even though I'm not sure why yet." The group should respect and support such a statement and should help the individual explore the reasons more. (This kind of exploration can be a fruitful experience that broadens the group's awareness, but it can also be overdone. Don't let every single second thought trip you up when you have thoroughly examined an issue and it is time to move ahead.)

It is also important to know what you actually think and feel about an issue when it comes to choosing a final decision. Identify which areas you can compromise or give up on, and don't get stuck defending them to the death for the sake of principle, or because you hate to give in. On the other hand, don't offer to compromise just to be a good sport in areas that are very important to you. If you agree to a decision unwillingly (or allow someone else to do so), you won't really be committed to the agreement, or you will carry around resentment that might cause trouble later.

10. Remember that at times, the best tool for constructive conflict is a little quiet time. It is important for people to express themselves during important discussions, but sometimes the atmosphere gets so argumentative that people are no longer listening to each other. At this point, try calling a break, asking for a few minutes' silence, suggesting that people count to ten before responding to a previous speaker, or in the case of an apparent deadlock, suggesting that the discussion stop and be picked up again at another time.

11. Finally, when normal meeting discussion doesn't seem sufficient to work out a conflict, you may want to set up a special, structured process for dealing with it. Schedule a special meeting, or even an all-day retreat, and use a neutral facilitator (either from

inside or outside the group) to help you through a program for dealing with the conflict. One such structured process, the "Creative Problem Solving Technique," is described in the following section.

### WAYS WE DON'T ACCEPT OBJECTIONS

Pressure is put on people to withdraw objections; people with objections are made to feel separate from the group; people are sometimes cross-examined in a hostile fashion about their objection; time is wasted arguing on whether an objection is right, rather than focusing on what can be done to meet it.

from INVERT

### CREATIVE PROBLEM SOLVING

The creative problem solving technique employs the basic principles useful in any good decision making process. Normally groups try to apply these methods in an informal way. But when a group is deadlocked in a conflict, or when an issue is so volatile that it is hard to use good decision-making techniques, a formalized, step-by-step process can provide a framework for approaching the situation in a constructive way.

Step 1: Set up a special meeting. The problem-solving process takes plenty of time, and it can't be rushed: don't expect it to be a short meeting. Call in someone to facilitate who is not personally involved in the conflict.

Step 2: Clear the air. If there is a great deal of hostility between the parties, this must be dealt with first. The process works most effectively when the conflicting parties trust one another; they must at least be committed to trying to meet each other's needs as well as their own. You may want to use some communication or interpersonal sensitivity exercises to build trust and understanding. *(Some exercises can be found in Chapter 11, TECHNIQUES FOR GROUP BUILDING, in the section entitled "Increase Involvement and Trust." Also see references mentioned at the end of this chapter.)*

Step 3: Define the problem. Define it as <u>shared</u>, not as the fault of, or belonging to, one "side" in the conflict. If you define a problem as shared, then the definition of a "successful" solution will be one that meets everyone's needs, rather than one that meets just your own.

Define the problem in terms of <u>needs</u>, not in terms of a solution. Define those needs as specifically as possible.

Example: To say, "We need to get more help from volunteers" is defining a solution. To say, "We have trouble getting everything done that we want to do," is defining a need. To say, "We have trouble getting the work power to do our monthly mailings and to clean up the building," is defining needs even more specifically.

There are several reasons for focusing on needs: a) it allows you to check out the legitimacy of the need (is it really so important? Is it a disguise for a different need?); b) it allows you creative freedom in searching for a solution, instead of following just one avenue; and c) it ensures that everyone is focusing on the same problem.

Step 4: Analyze the problem. Trace its history, the involvement of the parties concerned, people's feelings. Get as clear an understanding as possible. During this step you should still focus on sharing understanding, not arguing about who is right or wrong, and not pursuing solutions.

Step 5: Brainstorm solutions. By "brainstorm" we mean that everyone should offer every single idea she or he can think of for responding to the problem. Don't worry about whether ideas are good

## AN EXAMPLE OF PROBLEM SOLVING

Here is an example of how the problem-solving technique might be used in a specific situation. The imaginary problem involves a collective restaurant staff which is having trouble with their bookkeeper, Jerry. Most of the staff don't want to work with Jerry anymore and are asking him to leave. Jerry insists that they can't do this because the decision must be made by consensus and he, as a group member, blocks consensus on his own expulsion. A couple of other staff members support his right to do this. Feelings of anger, hostility and distrust are high.

Steps 1 and 2: Establishing the setting. The group sets up a special meeting to work on this problem. They invite a neutral facilitator, skilled in group process, to come in and guide them through the meeting. The first hour is spent expressing the mutual respect and trust they have for one another. They do some communications exercises to clarify their understanding of their feelings. Each person tries to remember one good experience she or he has had with Jerry in the last month. Jerry tries to think of positive experiences he has had with other members of the staff.

Step 3: Defining the problem. The problem is defined thus: Jerry and the other members of the staff have conflicting needs in the way they want to work. The other staff want to know what Jerry is doing, what decisions he is making, and how he is representing the group to outside people. Jerry wants to get his work done efficiently, without spending time consulting with people. He wants the rest of the collective to trust him and let him work independently.

Step 4: Analyzing the problem. Many strong feelings date from a particular incident where Jerry made an exception to the restaurant's food purchasing policy without consulting other staff members.

**81**

or bad, whether they will work or not. At this step, ideas should not be evaluated. The purpose of brainstorming is to create a criticism-free atmosphere that encourages people to be creative and to express all their ideas spontaneously. An idea that seems ridiculous may stimulate another one that is workable. Shoot for quantity rather than quality. Try to cover every possibility.

Step 6: Evaluate the solutions offered during the brainstorm. What needs does each one fill or not fill? What does implementation of different solutions involve? What are the outcomes of different courses of action? The criteria for evaluation should cover both logical, concrete considerations and also the feelings of the people involved. A good decision is one that is of high quality in its own right, but is also highly acceptable to those who must live with it.

Try to select, out of all the ideas proposed, the one that comes closest to meeting everyone's needs. Perhaps a creative new idea came up during the brainstorm that will completely satisfy everyone. If a single solution doesn't immediately jump out as "the answer," however, the group has resources to work with: a common understanding of needs, a knowledge of what solutions are possible, and a list of specific ideas to consider. Combine and reformulate these ideas and continue working toward finding a solution you can agree on. If the two parties trust each other and are committed to each other's needs, they will usually accept the solution which comes closest to satisfying all concerned.

Step 7: Once you reach agreement, remember to decide how the solution will be implemented, and how it will be reviewed and evaluated further down the road. Remember, too, that you need to take some time to pat yourselves on the backs and share good feelings about finally coming to agreement. You will deserve congratulations.

He was not aware of the historical reason for this policy. When others found out, they were angry.

Another dynamic that emerged was the difference in communication styles between Jerry and the rest of the group. The present problem was allowed to smolder for a long time because Jerry never talked to the others about his needs and feelings. Jerry feels uncomfortable talking about feelings and he feels that others are prying when they ask questions. His reaction to this situation is to withdraw, which others interpret as rejection and coldness on his part.

Step 5: Brainstorming. A few of the very many ideas generated include: Jerry leave the collective; Jerry stay and everyone else leave; Jerry try to change his style; other staff try to adjust to Jerry as he is; a compromise in which Jerry will agree to check all his decisions with one other person—Donna, with whom he has rapport. She will decide if the rest of the staff need to be consulted.

Step 6: Choosing a decision. The collective realized that they did not really dislike Jerry, but that they and Jerry were happier when they communicated and worked in different ways. Rather than rejecting Jerry, the group began to understand that he would be more satisfied in a different job situation.

Jerry recognized this as well. Rather than feeling rejected or discounted, he felt supported by the group because they were willing to understand and affirm the validity of what he needed in a working situation. He agreed he should look for another job. The group recognized that Jerry had valuable skills and they will give him good references and try to help him make contacts. Until he finds a job, he will remain with the collective.

On the surface, this decision appears to be the same as if the group had simply expelled Jerry, in accordance with their original intention. In fact, there is a great deal of difference. The final decision was not made in anger or mistrust, but from a cooperative position in which everyone tried to respond to everyone else's needs. The collective feels satisfied with this decision and believes it is the best one for all concerned. There are no carryover feelings of anger, resentment, or hostility.

Step 7: Wrapping up. Gary has volunteered to put Jerry in touch with several of the restaurant's regular customers who might be in a position to hire a good bookkeeper. A special meeting has been planned where Jerry will explain the specific frustrations of the bookkeeper's job to a few of the staff members so they can make plans that will make the job easier for future bookkeepers. The group plans to have a party to celebrate Jerry's new job as soon as he finds one he wants to take.

A second approach to dealing with conflicts in a structured way is one that comes from the Radical Therapy movement, and is best for interpersonal conflicts between individuals. This process, called "mediation," is fairly structured and can take from two to six hours in one or more sessions. Mediation uses many of the skills and principles discussed above, under the guidance of a neutral and trained third person.

We are presenting a brief outline of the mediation process because we feel that this chapter would be incomplete without at least some mention of the technique. We are convinced that the process can be an extraordinarily useful and powerful tool for interpersonal conflict resolution and problem solving. Mediation is a difficult process, however, and it confronts strong feelings. Before using it, we believe you should be trained by an experienced person. We recommend that

1

SUGGESTIONS FOR REORGANIZATION OF MANUAL..... ADDITIONAL SECTIONS + additions to handwritten sections

1. What is consensus? Why should we use consensus - here's where the advantages should be given. Then follow by explanation of why we have problems with it in this society. Then brief explanation of values on which consensus is based.

   Then, come back to values later on and intertwine them with how to put those values in practice. Values are no good - unless can be implemented; make them applicable to daily living.

2. Manual could be divided into two parts to give it some organization: Theory - including Introduction, Values inherent in Consensus, and Problems with Consensus, and advantages of consensus...and Practice - which contains the rest.

3. Do an introduction where we briefly refer to our values or reasons for doing the manual. Then go into definition, give background, do the step-by-step, go into some of the problems, and then return to an outright discussion of values. It might be much more convincing, more clear that one flows from the other.

4. We may want to omit talking about values separately at all, but to work them in as they come up naturally. It would be viable especially in the practicle section.

5. One other thought on the theory/practice idea: we could write it so that people could skp over the theory section if they wanted to.

6. Integrate our process through of developing this into the manual (chel has the specifics).

you do not try to follow the outline below in an attempt to do a mediation.
We do hope that this brief presentation
will encourage some readers to further
explore the process. *(See the reference
section at the end of this chapter.)*

A mediation is appropriate when relations among two or more people are
strained to the point that the individuals are having trouble working together. The people involved are willing
to negotiate toward some common goal, but
feelings of anger, hurt, or frustration
are interfering with their ability to do
their own problem solving. The goal of
mediation is to discuss the problem
openly, air the feelings, and agree to
specific behavioral changes. The mediator helps the people in conflict go
through the following steps.

1. Agree about the outcomes. Do you
both want to be here? Is the issue
really negotiable? Are your goals com-
patible?

2. Clear the air. Express all the
resentments that distort your communication with each other. The feelings
that come out are likely to be intense
and volatile; the mediator helps make
it safe to feel, express and hear the
hurt and angry feelings.

3. Check out assumptions. What are
your expectations and fears? Exchange
more information and clear more air.

4. Discuss perceptions of the problem. Talk about what you see happening.
Share insights and intuitions.

5. Do a mutual critique of the problem. Focus on a critical analysis of
the problem, not the other person. Each
person can also look at how her or his
own actions and behaviors contribute to
the situation.

6. Ask for what you want. This step
incorporates both "wishing for 100% of
what you want" and a friendly bargaining
approach. Explore all the possible options.

7. Make agreements about changes.
Make a "contract" to do things differently. Promise to work on specific behaviors that you both agree contribute
to the problem.

8. Share positive thoughts. Say what
you appreciate about each other and what
you like about each other, both in general and during this mediation session.

The mediation process can be extremely
helpful as a problem-solving tool for
people who are deadlocked in an interpersonal conflict. The mediator can make
a safe atmosphere in which to speak to
each other while encouraging the expression of strong feelings that have been
impeding progress in the relationship.

MOST HIGHLY RECOMMENDED RESOURCES

*INTERPERSONAL CONFLICT RESOLUTION* by Alan
    Filley

*"Mediations"* by Anita Friedman

*JOINING TOGETHER* by David and Frank
    Johnson

*"Ms."* Volume VII, No. 4, *"How to Handle
    Conflict"*

*BUILDING SOCIAL CHANGE COMMUNITIES,*
    Chapter 7, *"Creative Conflict Reso-
    lution,"* by The Training/Action
    Affinity Group

**84**

# Techniques for Group Building

Consensus decision making works best when the participants believe they belong to the group, and the group belongs to them. This group solidarity develops out of mutual trust and respect. As trust and respect grow within the group, members will feel free to express opinions and feelings, and to disagree without fear of consequences. Many consensus groups find that mutual caring is important to their sense of being a group, and they set aside time and plan activities to build friendships and develop a sense of community.

Members' ability and willingness to take responsibility for the group is another factor which contributes to the cohesiveness of groups. Taking responsibility means that each member contributes

to the functions of creating procedures and rules, supporting each other, defining goals, evaluating progress, and completing tasks. It is important for members to know they can influence the group.

Group building is the process by which group solidarity or cohesiveness develops. A group does not instantaneously come into being. It develops slowly over time. Every activity that is shared by group members, whether it is a business meeting, an office clean-up party, an anniversary picnic, or hours spent working together on a project, contributes to the group's sense of history and identity. In this sense, the group grows out of each member's contributions. In consensus groups it is particularly important that the group's growth be based on evolving norms of open communication, cooperation, and mutual trust and respect, since these norms support the values and skills of consensus. This chapter will discuss some factors which contribute to group solidarity and will describe some techniques which you can use in developing your group.

## TAKE YOUR GROUP SERIOUSLY

Individuals gather together for many reasons: sharing concerns, discussing philosophy, or working on a project. Some of these gatherings may evolve into groups. A group will emerge when its members think of themselves as a group. Two signs that a group has formed are: members representing themselves publically as a group; and choosing a group name. (For example, people living together cooperatively will often name their house.) A group identity helps to focus attention on what it means to be a part of the group.

A group is a creation of its members. It is important that group members spend time considering the nature of the group: What are the group's goals? How does it define membership? What are the rules for making decisions? If the rules and goals of a group develop out of a conscious and cooperative effort, rather than just "happening," then the group will express the will of its members. However, members must take the group seriously for this to occur.

Taking the group seriously involves more than accepting responsibility for choosing procedures and defining goals. It also includes showing care and respect for the group. Groups need special attention during transitions (when adding or losing members, when changing procedures or roles) to ensure that the changes contribute to the group's growth.

### Say Hello and Good-Bye

It is important to acknowledge new members when they enter the group as well as noting when someone leaves the group. A formal procedure for integrating new members helps them feel accepted and clarifies what is expected of them. Such a procedure also helps old members develop ties with newcomers. *(See the section below entitled "Help New Members Become Part of the Group.")*

When someone leaves the group, he or she should be expected to make the departure explicit rather than just "fading away." Explicit leavetakings make it clear that belonging to the group is something to be taken seriously and that members have a responsibility to each other to clarify their roles.

### Have Regular Evaluations

Set aside time at the end of every meeting (or on some regular basis) to talk about how the meeting went, how members feel about the process, and what might be done differently in the future. Evaluations help foster conscious group development since they: 1) give members a chance to affirm what they like about the group and each other; 2) offer an opportunity to clear up misunderstandings; 3) give members who were dissatisfied with the process a chance to be heard; 4) provide a time for planning improvements in the process to better meet the needs of the group; and 5) affirm that the group takes itself seriously since time is spent on the group's needs, not just projects.

When CCR held a meeting for an in-depth evaluation of our group process, we learned that we all had been working so hard on our group's tasks, and on serving other groups, that we were ignoring ourselves and getting out of touch with each other. We decided to call a temporary moratorium on accepting any new work and to focus instead on discussing internal issues and goals. We also used this time to emphasize our own "familial dimension." A committee was formed to develop ideas for bringing us all closer together. These suggestions included a "Resource Exchange" (everyone listed skills and resources they could share with other members of the group and the lists were copied and passed out), and small "Dinner Groups" of four people selected by drawing names from a hat. (These groups met for dinner or other purely social events over a period of a couple months.)

It is also helpful to occasionally set aside times for more in-depth evaluations. A group may want to evaluate how it worked on a specific project, how it has worked over the past six months or year, or whether politics, goals or methods need to be refined. *(See the "Evaluations" section in Chapter 6, STRUCTURING YOUR MEETINGS, for suggestions about how to conduct an evaluation.)*

## SHARE RESPONSIBILITY

Members are most committed to a group when they feel they are making an important contribution, not just being led. It is important to make sure that every member has a chance to be active in the group and to influence the direction that the group takes. Members also need to feel that other members are taking active responsibility and can be depended upon.

### Balance Participation in Group Tasks

If a few members carry most of the weight in a group while others feel helpless or left out, there are specific techniques a group can use to equalize participation. Usually the members who are assuming more than their share of responsibility are eager to find a way to distribute that responsibility more evenly, even if they don't know how to make this change. Start by analyzing why certain people end up doing more. Do they have access to more information or do they have more experience than other people? Do contacts from outside the group repeatedly turn to certain individuals as representatives of the group? Do members automatically look to certain people for leadership? Do less active members lack confidence?

These patterns can be broken. Redistribute tasks or information flow so different people can get in the center of what's going on. Send new faces to represent the group at the next press conference or coalition meeting. Make

INFORMATION POWER

"In one group we know of, the bookkeeper had a disproportionate amount of power at meetings because, given her knowledge of the group's financial situation, other members had to rely on her opinion during meetings about whether certain decisions were financially feasible or not. The books were not kept in a place where other members could gain access to this information, so the power imbalance was continued."

87

an effort in meetings to get different people to talk, and <u>listen</u> to what they say. Set up a time for <u>in-services</u>, when a member with a special skill or expertise can teach what he or she knows to other group members.

## Balance Participation at Meetings

It's a rare group in which each member is equally involved in each meeting. Different degrees of interest, information, or styles of communication will result in different levels of input during meetings. Ideally, though, every member should feel involved and free to contribute. No one should dominate or monopolize, and no one should be left out. Following are some guidelines and techniques you can use to balance participation in meetings.

--Rotate roles such as notetaker, facilitator, or other roles your group may have established. This allows different people to share in leadership and encourages everyone to develop a variety of skills.

--Try to sit in a circle whenever possible so everyone can have eye contact with everyone else. Circles tend to encourage more balanced participation and prevent anyone from being at the "head" of the group physically.

--If some individuals consistently tend to dominate discussion, you can limit time per speaking turn, or limit number of speaking turns per discussion. Sometimes groups give each participant a pile of matchsticks; each speaking turn requires "payment" of a matchstick, thus limiting each person's number of contributions. Another technique is to pass a token from hand to hand, giving the right to speak only to the holder. At CCR we have tried passing an egg timer from speaker to speaker to encourage concise, focused contributions.

--If some members are less assertive, or participate less, you can use a "round "robin," giving each member a turn to state his or her opinion (with option to

pass). In addition, the techniques of brainstorming and the "travelling chair" can promote balanced participation. *(See the section entitled "Doing Discussion" in Chapter 6, STRUCTURING YOUR MEETINGS, for a fuller explanation of these techniques.)*

Even with the above techniques, perfect balance in participation is unlikely to occur. Some people are simply more verbal than others. When group members get to know who just naturally says a lot and who only speaks up when it seems crucially important, then members can make adjustments for individual differences.

> Example: The group may know that Gregg is shy and needs encouragement to speak; Laura doesn't say much, but can be counted on to get her point across when she's ready; Paul usually speaks a lot and his reticence on a particular occasion probably has some significance which should be investigated; and Vera needs feedback after she presents an idea or she will keep talking until Doomsday.

Since participation in the group will be uneven, it is important for the members to watch for patterns or consistencies in imbalances. Do the women regularly say less than the men? Do new members participate less than older, established members? Do young or middle-aged members say less? Do people who have money invested in the group say more? Such consistencies, which often reflect societal norms, may indicate incipient problems for the group. It is easy to assume that Karen, Sue and Deborah are quiet in meetings because of the particular personal styles of these three individuals: it might be more difficult, but accurate, to recognize that women speak less in your group than men. Such patterns can be the result of societal conditioning which is often so subtle that participants aren't aware of it. Perhaps women speak less in your group because they have been taught to be unassertive, or because they have unconsciously realized that when they do speak, their contributions carry less weight than those of male members. Imbalances such as this should be brought up at evaluation time so people can share insights and talk about how to deal with them.

One group we've heard of developed a technique for slowing down fast-paced arguments and for equalizing the imbalance in assertiveness between men and women, which was a problem in their group. After a speaker had finished talking, women members had to count to five before they could respond. Men had to count to ten.

In consensus, decisions are made by talking about an issue until agreement is reached. Therefore, verbal skills and the confidence to use those skills are essential. Lack of skills or confidence can be responsible for both under-participation and over-participation at meetings. Members may be afraid to take the risk of speaking up, or they may speak incessantly because they are afraid they are not being heard and understood. In both cases, the members' ability to contribute to the group is decreased. The group as a whole is responsible for creating a supportive atmosphere and en-suring opportunities for all members to learn necessary skills.

Both under-participating and over-participating members can be assisted in improving their skills. Make it clear what you want them to learn to do and encourage a group atmosphere that sup-ports their learning to change rather than being intimidating or critical. One way to help under-participating mem-bers is to ask specific questions when you think their contribution would be of value.

Example: You might say, "Dan, when we were having lunch yesterday, you made a good observation about our group process. Would you mind explaining it to the whole group?" -- "Valerie, I've heard what everyone thinks about my proposal except you. I really want to know your opinion."

Let people know when their comments have been valuable, and give them feedback that will help improve their skills.

Example: "Ann, I realize we all re-sponded defensively when you criti-cized our newsletter, and that made it hard for us to be open to what you were saying. I think we would have responded better if you had started out by saying you had a few ideas about how to improve the newsletter, rather than saying it was no good as it is now."

The most helpful feedback describes spe-cific behaviors to change.

Example: Instead of blaming Clara for her long, rambling comments, a member could say, "Clara, next time, before you speak, try stopping to think pre-cisely what point you want to make. Then make that clear first thing. That way we won't be confused or frus-trated trying to follow your thoughts. (See "Feedback and Criticism" in Chap-ter 8, COMMUNICATION SKILLS.)

You can also help people during discus-sions.

Example: You can say, "Ben, are you saying you are worried about the bad press this project might get us? Thank you for bringing that up--it's an important point to consider." This type of statement can cut through meandering comments and help Ben see a precise way to make his point. At the same time, the importance of Ben's contribution is acknowledged.

Developing better communication skills is a shared concern of the group. An individual who feels blamed for a prob-lem and who is left alone with the re-sponsibility for learning to change, will probably not change at all. In-dividuals need emotional support and constructive feedback from the group in order to behave differently. It is im-portant to remember that the process of helping individuals change strengthens the group as a whole.

**89**

## ENCOURAGE SOCIAL INTERACTION

During its development, every group must go through an initial period of social interaction in which members get to know each other as individuals apart from the task of the group. In addition, every meeting usually begins with a period of social time where people catch up with each other and reaffirm their relationships. It is wise to recognize the necessity of such interaction and build it into your group's life: allow time for friendship as well as for work. Below are some techniques for channeling social energy into your group building process.

### At the Beginning of Meetings

People need time to talk personally with each other before beginning business matters. If members arrive at 7 o'clock, don't expect business to begin until 7:10 or even later. It just won't happen, and if people are forced to start working without any social time, they will probably get distracted by social interaction during business.

Some groups actually acknowledge this social time by having two meeting times, one for "gathering," perhaps including dinner or refreshments, and a second time for business to begin. You may also want to formalize this interaction time within the context of the meeting. If the group is meeting for the first time, begin with introductions. An ongoing group should repeat this process whenever new members attend meetings: it makes the new people feel recognized and welcomed, and it can serve as a basis for getting acquainted later. For ongoing groups, a check-in procedure is often valuable. Each member takes a few moments to tell how they are, what they have been doing since the last meeting, something they are excited about, or other anecdotes. This technique has the added advantage of uncovering "hidden agendas" in advance. (Gary can warn the group that he has a headache and may be irritable.)

**90**

### Build Fun Into Meetings

Having fun together can bring group members closer together, if fun is structured in such a way that it doesn't completely disrupt the business of the meeting. In addition to ice cream breaks, meeting at the swimming pool, or any other sources of fun you can come up with, you may want to try "Light and Livelies." These are quick, playful activities that can wake people up and break up tension or monotony. Some examples include:

--Group Stretch: Everyone stands and follows the motions of a leader.

--Magic Blob: An imaginary, protean "blob" is passed around the circle. Each person takes it from the previous person in one shape, but passes it to the next person in a new form. For example, when John passes the blob to Cathy, it is a piece of stretchy taffy. In Cathy's

"Somebody in our local Movement for a New Society group here told one meeting about another MNS group that had established a 'frivolity committee' whose task was to make spontaneous light and lively interventions during meetings. While we did not establish a formal frivolity committee here, several of us quietly took on this task for one of our monthly meetings. During the middle of one of our meetings, we unexpectedly got bogged down in a very heavy and time-consuming decision-making discussion. Without announcement, three of us leaped to our feet and began to sing (and act out) the first verse of the 'Hokey-Pokey.' The other participants were startled and also leaped to their feet without thinking about what was happening. Within seconds, the entire group was doing the 'Hokey-Pokey.' The activity finished, we resumed our discussion with our heads more clear and with a sense of freshness in our interactions."

--Jim Struve

hands it turns into a bouncing ball.
But when Gary catches the ball on a
dribble, it becomes a very heavy bar-
bell.

--Touch Blue:  The group stands together.  When the game leader shouts,
"touch blue," everyone must find something blue on another person and touch
it as quickly as possible.  Then "touch
purple," "touch polka dots," "touch a
leather belt," "touch curly hair."

--Human Pretzels:  The group stands
in a circle.  Each person reaches across
the circle with both hands (not crossed)
and grasps hands with two different
people.  Then, without letting go, try
to untangle.  If you are lucky, you may
find yourselves in a reassembled circle
with everyone holding hands with the
person next to them.

--Role Playing:  Agenda items do not
always have to be presented in a serious,
factual manner.  People can take on
roles and act out reports to the group,
problems for discussion, etc.  Role playing provides some comic relief to the
meeting and puts things back in perspective when they have become overly serious.

## Get Together Just for Fun

Picnics, potlucks, volleyball games, etc.,
are a good way to bring together socially
people who normally meet just to do work.
Such gatherings help members become
friends as well as co-workers and increase their sense of involvement with
the group.  These gatherings are also a
good time to meet each others' friends
and families and to visit each other's
homes.


## INCREASE INVOLVEMENT AND TRUST

Throughout this manual, we stress the
importance of trust among members of a
group.  Trust is a difficult quality to
build in its own right.  It usually develops only after group members have
shared activities together which increase
their mutual understanding, caring and
respect.  Group members don't have to
always be in agreement to trust each
other.  However members do need to know
that, despite differences, others will
respect them, will be fair with them,
and will care about their feelings.

The more that communication occurs between members, and the better they get to know each other, the better the chance of developing trust. Following are a few specific exercises that your group can use to increase mutual understanding, and to give members an opportunity to develop the personal relationships you already have with each other. Many other activities are described in the references at the end of this chapter.

## Reflections

Divide into pairs. Pairs may work separately, or they may work with another pair, each pair observing the other to increase members' opportunities for learning more about each other.

A facilitator should provide a simple, but personal question. (E.g., "What do I value about this group?" "What are my frustrations with this group?" "Where do I want to be five years from now?" "How do I feel about changes I see happening in this group, this city, the world?")

Now one member (Paul) should answer the question as he thinks his partner (Claudia) would answer it. Claudia should listen to Paul, then tell him how his answer is like or different from what her answer really would have been. The two participants may want to have an informal discussion about why Paul drew certain conclusions, how Claudia felt about hearing them, or how Paul felt about guessing right or wrong.
Then reverse roles and have Claudia tell Paul what she thinks his answer to the question would be.

--Variation I: Use the above exercise in relation to a difficult issue or disagreement in the group. For example, in preparation for problem solving about a conflict between Claudia and Paul, the exercise can help each person understand the other's perspective better and identify potential misunderstandings.

--Variation II: This exercise can be adapted to practice paraphrasing.

Claudia gives her own answer to the question, then Paul restates, in his own words, what he believes Claudia said. This activity develops good listening skills and increases members' awareness of the communication problems which can arise when a speaker's statement is misunderstood.

## Dyadic Risk Taking (Adapted from Pfeiffer and Jones)

Divide into pairs. Paul tells Claudia something personal about himself. It can be an extremely risky disclosure (something that is hard to reveal), or it can be very safe (something easy to talk about), or somewhere in between. Paul might say, "I have a dog named Pepper," "I have $700 in the bank," "I am ashamed of my voice and I try to avoid situations where I would be expected to sing," or "Last week I spent a whole evening reading a Gothic novel."

Now Claudia makes a judgment about how risky the statement was for Paul to make (0 = no risk; 1 = minimal risk; 2 = mild risk; and 3 = a pretty big risk). Claudia writes down her score and does not show it to Paul.

Then Claudia makes a personal statement and Paul records the amount of risk he judges that statement to be.

After each person has made five statements, they show each other the risk scores and discuss their perceptions with each other. Why were certain statements risky and others not? Were there any big differences between what the two people thought was risky? What are the reasons for these differences? Did it become more or less risky to make statements as the exercise proceeded? Why?

Hints: It helps to sit side-by-side so members can regulate how much they want to look at each other during the exercise. Also, during the exercise, participants should not respond to each other's statements, but merely score them and then make a statement of their own.

**92**

## Positive Feedback

Each member receives a slip of paper or index card for every other member of the group. Participants are instructed to write a positive statement or "message of happiness" for each group member on the separate slips of paper. Some guidelines are: 1) write messages that begin with "I" ("I like . . ." -- "I feel . . ."); 2) be specific ("I like the way you smile at everyone," rather than, "I like your attitude."); 3) write a special message to fit each person rather than a comment that could apply to several people. Members can sign their messages or leave them anonymous.

Each participant designates a certain place as their "mailbox" and people distribute their messages to the appropriate boxes.

When all messages have been delivered and read, participants are invited to share feedback that was most meaningful to them, clarify any ambiguous messages, and express the feelings they have experienced during the process.

--Variation: Instead of written messages, members could be asked to bring small, meaningful presents for each other to some meeting or special occasion.

## Most Precious Possession

This exercise could begin or end a regular meeting, or it might be part of a special session for building group communication. Each member brings their "most precious possession" and, without showing it to the others, places it in a box designated for this purpose.

Later, each item is taken out, one by one, and the group tries to guess who the object belongs to. After the objects have all been taken out and guesses made, owners claim their objects and tell the group why they are precious. Participants are encouraged to talk about their feelings and what they have learned about each other and themselves.

--Variation I: Instead of objects, you may want to use drawings that people have made, pictures cut out from magazines that members feel are meaningful or expressive of themselves, verses of poetry, quotations, names of famous people who have been a source of inspiration, etc.

--Variation II: Members might instead bring some symbolic object that they want to get rid of (the blue jeans that are too big since you finally lost weight, the resume you used job hunting in an area of work you have decided to give up, etc.). After sharing the objects with each other, you might want to build a bonfire and burn them. This could be a joyful activity celebrating positive changes you are making in your lives.

## Trust Walk

Members pair up. One partner is blindfolded and the second partner leads him or her on a walk outside. The sighted partner makes sure that the blindfolded one is safe and does not stumble or bump into anything, trying to reassure the blindfolded person if he or she is nervous. Then trade roles. Afterwards, members talk with each other about how the exercise felt.

---

Mikal writes re: p. 9/a....

The intro. is a bit moralistic for my taste. I would emphasize Cons. as a process oriented towards a wbold new _class_ or problems -- _hisorically_ generated -- namely, ones demanding solutions for which there is no traditional model. Hence creativity demanded.

93

## HELP NEW MEMBERS
## BECOME PART OF THE GROUP

Providing a framework for new people to become fully integrated members is an important concern for any group. It is an especially sensitive issue in groups which make decisions by consensus because in such groups each member has a great deal of power to affect the actions of the rest of the group. This individual power is the reason we think consensus is a good process. However there can be trouble when a new member is inexperienced with consensus and doesn't yet know how to use it well. Even if a new member is familiar with consensus, lack of knowledge about the group, its history and its goals, could cause problems. For this reason, many groups which use consensus are cautious about who they allow to join or how they integrate new members. Your group should seriously consider: Who can be a member and how will new members be integrated into the group? What will we do to give new members the skills and the knowledge they need to participate well?

It is important to consider how new members develop a sense of belonging and acceptance in the group. New members need to feel wanted and welcomed. They need to be given access to information they will need to participate in the group so they can feel like "insiders." (Where are materials kept in the office? Why do we always meet on the East Side of town? What is that "in" joke about MacDonald's? Who is Howie Drewick and why does everyone growl when his name is mentioned? Why is a procedure done this way instead of that other, obviously more efficient way?)

If older members don't make an effort to become acquainted with new members and to incorporate them into the group, then the experience of being new can be frustrating, lonely and alienating. For example, if clear guidelines for appropriate group behavior are not available, then new members can only learn by making mistakes, by violating group norms and

procedures. This can lead to a steady stream of negative comments from older to newer members--a situation likely to convince newcomers they are unwelcome or inept. New members can also be bewildered by being told of a "rule," and then seeing other members break that rule. They need to know when, how and why certain regulations are sometimes ignored.

Even when new members are welcomed, it can be difficult for older members to give them the necessary time and support. Older members are busy with the group's work and with their friendships with each other. It can be difficult to spend adequate time with new people. Also, it's hard to know how to relate to an unknown quantity.

Without realizing it, older members might perceive new members as a threat to group stability. A new member might bring change to a group which older members love, or understand, just the way it is. A complaint we heard from a new member at CCR was, "Every time I suggest a new idea, someone says, 'Oh, we tried that two years ago." I feel like people aren't open to considering what I have to offer." It is easy to assume that because someone is new, he or she doesn't have anything valuable to.give the group yet. Sometimes, however, a person will have a creative idea or a fresh perspective just because they have a different background of experiences than the one shared by the older group members. It is a mistake to discount these new ideas (or revitalized old ideas) too quickly.

There are specific things your group can do to facilitate the process of bringing in new members. These suggestions may not make the experience easy for newcomers, but they can clarify what is expected of new members and what new members can expect of the group. Your process may also include a specific procedure for phasing out new members if they don't work out. Following are a few ideas.

**94**

> I found myself frustrated because I was doing the greater part of the
> clerical work in the office. One of the reasons I was getting stuck with this
> work (a process in which I also played a part), was that I knew better than others
> how to do this work: where things were kept, all the little details, etc. To
> get myself out of this role, and to enable others to do it, I wrote an "Office
> Procedures Manual" about how to do everything in the office. Some people never
> used it, but a lot of people did and it had the effect I'd wanted of freeing me
> from so much of this responsibility. But later a new member to the group told
> me (in a nice way) that she thought this book was an instrument of oppression.
> Whenever she asked group members where to find something, or how to do something,
> instead of responding to her in a personal way, they would brush her off, saying,
> "Look in the Procedures Manual." I like this example a lot for several reasons:
> It illustrates a good sol. to equalizing info. (+ power) & for changing established
> patterns. It also shows how a good sol. can become a "bad" one
> w/o the group even being aware of it ∴ it shows the need for constant reexamination
> of procedures./procedures) habits ( also illustrate the value of new perceptions of
> new people — dynamic

1. Introduce new members at meetings. Let them say why they are interested in the group, what they want from it, what they can give it. The more old members know about the new ones, the more basis they will have for trying to get to know them. Make a point, also, to introduce all the old members to a new member.

2. Formalize the process of extending information to new people. Have a special orientation session for them. Or have something written for new people which tells about the group and how to perform various task functions.

3. Provide each new member with a "buddy"--someone who will take extra trouble to help out, someone to go to with questions, someone other members can go through if they want to give feedback to the new member and don't know him or her well enough yet to do it more directly.

4. Try bringing new members in in bunches, or "flocks." Two, three or four new people can give each other support and work through the period of strangeness together.

5. At CCR, a new member is an "intern" for the first three months. An intern has the same responsibilities as other group members and takes part in decision-making discussions. But he or she cannot block consensus. After the internship period, there is an evaluation for the intern at one of the regular staff meetings. (Most interns ask for this evaluation: they feel a need for feedback from the group, want a chance to give their own feedback, and this step formalizes the group's recognition of the new person as an integrated member. Older members may also ask for an evaluation at this time.) After the evaluation, the intern usually "flies up" to full membership. Occasionally someone may be asked to remain an intern awhile longer, or to leave. But if a new member isn't working out with the group, he or she usually loses interest and leaves during the internship.

6. You might want to have a "clearness meeting" to explore with a new person why he or she wants to be in the group, what mutual expectations are, and how to deal with any anticipated problems. Such a meeting could be held when

a person first considers joining a group, at the end of an internship period, or both.

7. Have scheduled check-ins or updates with new people. Ask them how they are feeling about their role in the group. What do they need from other members to make things easier?

## MOST HIGHLY RECOMMENDED RESOURCES

"The Agony of Inequality" by Jane J. Mansbridge in CO-OPS, COMMUNES AND COLLECTIVES by John Case and Rosemary Taylor, eds.

RESOURCE MANUAL FOR A LIVING REVOLUTION by Virginia Coover, et al.

"The Bases of Social Power" by J.R.P. French and B. Raven in STUDIES IN SOCIAL POWER by D. Cartwright, ed.

THE NEW GAMES BOOK by Andrew Fluegelman, ed.

FOR THE FUN OF IT! by Marta Harrison

JOINING TOGETHER by David and Frank Johnson

A HANDBOOK OF STRUCTURED EXPERIENCES FOR HUMAN RELATIONS TRAINING by J. William Pfeiffer and John Jones, eds.

CLEARNESS by Peter Woodrow

I would like to regularize our pronoun usage — with her or his, she or he, etc. Always putting female first. (Consciousness raising is never all done.)

Rewrite to eliminate phrase "our ideas." We're trying to get away from individual ownership of ideas and most of "our stuff" isn't new.

God, this is good! Good stuff! Thanks for all yr energy. Crps

# Chapter 12

# Adaptations of the Process for Special Situations

The consensus process described so far works best in small, homogeneous groups where members share common goals and values, have a high level of trust, and have plenty of time and patience. Consensus can sometimes work effectively in other situations, however--in large, diverse groups of people and under tight time constraints.

In large groups, the sheer numbers of participants may prevent everyone from having a say in a meeting of the whole group. The use of small groups for part of the discussion, and using representatives, can facilitate decision making so that many of the advantages of "pure" consensus decision making can be preserved.

Even when the group is small, time pressures can sometimes make full blown consensus decision making impossible. In such cases, provisions for an "escape clause" for voting, or special techniques for speeding the decision along may allow the group to keep some of the important elements of consensus. In this chapter we will describe some techniques for adapting the consensus process in special situations.

## FORMALIZED PROCESS

When the group is large, when time is tight, or when the subject being discussed is highly controversial or emotional, the group may want to use a formal structure for the discussion. In such cases, the facilitator plays a strongly directive role, determines who speaks when, and exercises rigid constraints on the discussion, making sure that only pertinent issues are discussed and that all talk is succinct and to the point. Some specific techniques for formalized process are described below.

## Stacking

Members wishing to speak must raise their hands and the facilitator acknowledges them in order. For instance, if five people raise their hands at once, the facilitator might say, "Karen first, then Don, Anna, Joan, and Steve." As these people speak, others wanting turns raise their hands and the facilitator puts their names on a mental or written list, then indicates in order whose turn is next. Often two people will want to make the same point, so when it comes to Steve's turn, he may just say, "I was going to say what Anna said," or "I pass."

An advantage of stacking is that participation is well equalized. However the issues raised may not get the discussion they need when it is appropriate. When a discussion is heated, sometimes people become so eager to speak or respond to each other that it becomes difficult to attend to what other people are saying. In such situations you might want to use a further variation of stacking which allows limited back-and-forth discussion to proceed after each person in the stack speaks. This discussion must be guided by directive facilitation (possibly using two facilitators) so it doesn't get out of control. After the limited exchange, the facilitator calls on the next person in the stack.

Even during ordinary stacking, it is sometimes necessary to interrupt the regular flow of turn taking. Such interruptions are allowed when a member has some information unknown to the rest of the group that is relevant to what another speaker is saying. (The point must be strictly informational, not opinion, and it should be immediately relevant and necessary to the discussion.) The person with the information says to the facilitator, "I have a point of information," and is allowed to interject that information, briefly and concisely, before the group returns to the turn-taking sequence.

Similarly, it may sometimes be necessary to interrupt the stacking process with a

"point of process," such as, "I think the group should know, we only have ten minutes left," or "This discussion is getting too personal. We have to get back to the issue."

## Using Silence

It is often helpful for the facilitator to call for a moment of silence so group members can slow down a heated exchange. By interrupting such an interaction, silence can help people remember that it isn't necessary to respond to every statement they disagree with, and it isn't necessary to repeat points that have been stated earlier. It is necessary, though, for all important viewpoints to be aired in a calm atmosphere where everything said will be remembered and considered.

## Time Limits

Another technique for formalizing and speeding up discussion in large groups, or when an issue is volatile, is to have time limits for how long each person may speak. For instance, the facilitator may allow everyone who wants to make a statement to do so, but with a limitation of two minutes. Such limits force speakers to be concise, to emphasize only what is most important, and not to get drawn into long, rhetorical arguments or rebuttals of previous speakers.

## Proposals and Amendments

In a more casual situation, decisions will often "evolve" out of discussion. In formal situations, or when discussion seems to be scattered over a number of issues so that areas of agreement aren't clear, a group member may, at some point, make a specific proposal.

> Example: "I propose we go ahead and hire John for three months and make one of the duties of his job to be trying to find funding to hire two more people after the summer."

A proposal of this kind is best made only after some discussion of the issue has occurred, most viewpoints and relevant information have been aired, and the time seems right to organize the group's thoughts into a decision. After the proposal is made, more discussion should occur as the group reacts to it. If the reaction seems positive, the facilitator may ask, "Are there any objections to this proposal?" If there are not, the decision is final. (Make sure the proposal is repeated fully, so members are sure about what they are agreeing to.)

A member may be willing to accept a proposal with minor alterations and may offer a "friendly amendment."

> Example: "I can go along with the proposal, but I'd like to add the stipulation that after six weeks we have a meeting with John to review the work he is doing and how things are working out. At that time we may decide to change the terms of his employment."

## Straw Votes

Straw voting is an informal, non-binding show of hands to test the number of people in a group who support a particular decision. The technique is controversial among those who use consensus. Some people feel that any kind of voting may become a form of tyranny by numbers or may be used to single out dissenters and put pressure on them. However there are some advantages of straw voting in certain situations that may justify its use. First, in extremely large groups, it is often difficult to tell whether long, drawn-out discussion represents serious disagreement, or if participants are merely raising all the issues and expressing opinions. A straw vote may be used to estimate how close the group is to consensus, and whether it is time to start struggling to finalize a decision, or whether much more discussion is necessary. Secondly, in large groups, many people do not have a turn to speak. A straw vote is a way for silent people to express their opinions and feel that they are being given a chance to have input. If this technique is used, the

facilitator should make it clear that the straw vote is _not_ a change to majority rule, but merely a way of testing the current state of agreement or disagreement in the group, and of identifying the most serious objections for further discussion.

## Multiple Facilitators

In the kinds of situations described in this chapter, the role of facilitator can be highly demanding, requiring close attention and vigilance. In such cases, it is especially useful to have two facilitators. One may act as timekeeper while the other plays process observer, or one may handle stacking, while the other attends to clarifying the subject being discussed. If one facilitator gets tired or becomes emotionally embroiled, the second can step in and provide support.

## A Word on Versatility

Many groups vacillate between the formal process described here and a more easygoing, informal process. The facilitator of a particular meeting may play an unobtrusive, back-seat role when things are going smoothly, but may step forward and offer more formalized direction when it seems needed. It is helpful for groups to be skilled in both informal and formal process and to have the versatility to switch back and forth as the situation demands.

## REPRESENTATIVE CONSENSUS DECISION MAKING

Sometimes a group of hundreds of people can operate by consensus using a representative method. The Clamshell Alliance (an anti-nuclear action coalition) uses a method that involves dividing a very large group into small units known as "affinity groups." Affinity groups consist of eight to 15 people who work together closely over a period of time. They develop the mutual trust and understanding and the common knowledge and experiences necessary for good consensus decision making. When the larger group needs to make a decision, each of the affinity groups meets and discusses the matter (see diagram). Each affinity group sends a representative (known as a "spoke") to a "spokes meeting." This meeting of representatives discusses the issue and comes up with one or more proposals. The spokes then return to their affinity groups where the proposal is discussed. Then spokes go back to the spokes meeting with feedback from their groups and acceptance or rejection of the proposal.

To finalize a decision, the spokes must reach consensus. Each spoke represents a group which in turn must come to consensus on what decision it wants its spoke to support. Therefore, each person in the large group has a chance to block consensus within the affinity group and through the group's spoke. If a proposal of the spokes meeting is rejected, the matter is discussed again, the reasons for rejection are aired, and a new pro-

posal is developed. The back-and-forth process between meetings of affinity groups and spokes meetings continues until consensus is reached. This process is long and arduous, but it ensures that decisions represent input from everyone in the group. Reaching a decision sometimes takes many hours, but people who have used this method have generally found it worth the trouble.

## THE MAJORITY RULE ESCAPE CLAUSE

Many groups which prefer to make most of their decisions by consensus have an alternative process in reserve--a majority rule "escape clause"--which can be used when consensus fails to produce a decision quickly enough for the needs of the group. We will describe some of these procedures below and then briefly address the arguments for and against having such an escape clause.

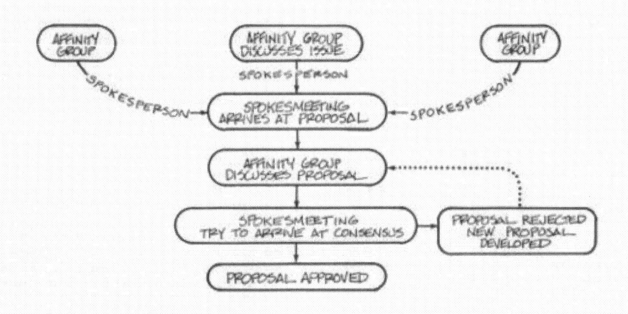

REPRESENTATIVE CONSENSUS DECISION MAKING

*The Majority Rule Escape Hatch*

## Martha's Rules of Order

This method comes from a paper entitled, *"Suggestions for Harmonious Meetings,"* affectionately known as "Martha's Rules of Order." It was developed by a cooperative household called "Martha's" in Madison, Wisconsin. The purpose of the process is stated: "We recognize that consensus decision making, while it takes a lot of time, makes for high quality decisions. But some decisions are not worth the effort. So we developed a way to decide whether or not an issue was important enough to warrant taking the extra time to reach consensus."

After an issue is discussed, a formal proposal is presented, and a preliminary show of hands is called for:

--Who likes the proposal?

--Who can live with the proposal?

--Who is uncomfortable with the proposal?

If no one is uncomfortable, the decision is implemented. If some members are uncomfortable, they are asked to state why and there is a discussion. Then a vote is taken on the following question:

"Should we implement this decision over the stated objections of the minority, when a majority of the people in the house feel it is workable?"

A "yes" vote leads to majority rule. A "no" vote means postponing the decision until consensus can be reached through further discussion.

## The Bailly Method

This method was used by the Bailly Alliance of Chicago, a former anti-nuclear group in the Midwest. When consensus could not be reached, members would vote on whether to revert to majority rule. A three-fourths majority was necessary in order to revert to voting, and a three-fourths majority was necessary to finalize any decision when this happened.

## Elaine's Alternative

A more elaborate process with a similar "escape" goes like this:

1. The group reaches consensus on the definition of the problem before discussing solutions.

2. An ample but defined time period is set for airing and discussing the proposals, including questions and clarification.

3. When major objections arise, the group breaks into small groups for the purpose of creating amendments, resolutions or new proposals. Participants then return to the larger group to discuss, prioritize, and select resolutions.

4. If there is still no consensus, the objectors are asked if they will step aside and allow the decision to be adopted if:

--Their dissenting ideas are recorded.

--It is stipulated that the decision does not set a precedent and cannot be used as a basis for future decisions.

**101**

--It is implemented for a trial period, with a well-defined set of criteria for evaluation.

5. If the objectors refuse, a committee is formed containing an equal number of members representing each opinion. The committee's assignment is to develop a new proposal within a set period of time. Their proposal is brought back to the group for a final decision.

6. If consensus cannot be reached on the new proposal, then the group tries to reach consensus to go to a three-fourths majority vote.

7. As a very last resort, three-fourths of the group may vote to decide by a three-fourths majority vote.

## Pros and Cons of the Escape Clause

We conclude these descriptions of the majority rule escape clause with the following points. On the positive side one can say that in most groups the "clause" is rarely used, and that it takes off some of the pressure the group feels by knowing that they must come to full consensus. Time pressures are, after all, one of the realities that a group must deal with, and sometimes the escape clause provides the group with a legitimate response to time problems. Especially when the group is inexperienced with consensus and is having difficulties working with it, an escape clause may be the only way of avoiding frustrations that would lead them to abandon consensus altogether.

On the other hand, some believe that time pressure is often good for a group since it forces members to learn to work together well enough to use consensus on a regular basis. When an escape clause exists, those in the majority position may be tempted to take the easy way out rather than giving serious consideration to the opinions of those in the minority.

THE MINORITY RULE ESCAPE CLAUSE

The Wisconsin Womyn's Land Cooperative, a living and recreational farm for women and children, uses consensus. But they have also developed a special conflict resolution procedure for addressing issues of strongly diverse opinions, and for formulating difficult policy decisions. The procedure includes pre-meeting preparations for individuals, in which women explore their own perspectives, contradictions, and interests. Then the special conflict resolution meeting is held, using principles of consensus, criticism/self-criticism, and maximum participation.

The unique feature of the process is the "Provision of Last Resource." If, after thoroughly discussing and exploring the issues, no consensus can be reached, the decision is delegated to a smaller group of people. The subgroup members must represent all the perspectives, and they are chosen and agreed to by all. They must be ongoing organization members, well versed in consensus and criticism skills, and they are expected to be flexible and to change in the course of their further work together. No later substitutions are allowed for those assigned to the small group. These women

**102**

meet until they reach consensus, and their decision is binding for the whole group.

A potential problem with this method is that without very thorough reporting to the large group of both the con-

tent and process of the small group's work, some members of the larger group may not be satisfied by or even understand the final decision. An advantage, however, is that it does allow a thorough attack on the problem: representatives of all positions work until opposing views are resolved into

## FORC MEETING PROCESS

The procedure below is adapted from a process developed by the Federation of Ohio River Cooperatives for use in large organizational meetings.

1. A proposal is presented to the entire group.

2. The large group breaks into small groups which "buzz," or quickly talk, to bring up any questions necessary to clarify the proposal.

3. A meeting of the large group polls representatives of the small groups for clarifying questions and answers are provided.

4. One minute of silence is allowed for participants to consider the proposal

5. The small groups meet to discuss the proposal. Do participants want to accept it, offer friendly amendments, voice strong disagreements or major objections?

6. In the large group, the small groups are polled for their reactions. If there is a major objection, proceed to step 7, if not, skip to step 8.

7. a. Small groups buzz to come up with suggestions to resolve objections, or with further creative suggestions.

    b. The large group polls the small group for results of 7.a.

    c. Again, small groups buzz for one minute about their reactions to ideas expressed during 7.b.

    d. In the large group, facilitators ask whether objections have been met by the suggestions made above.

3. Small groups talk again to consider members' feelings about the proposal and added suggestions. Facilitators join groups where objections exist.

8. In the large group, concerns are prioritized and amendments combined to produce a new proposal.

9. Small groups buzz for clarifying questions about the proposal developed under Step 8.

10. In the large group a poll is taken for clarifying questions, and answers are given.

11. Small groups discuss whether they can support the proposal as revised.

12. There is a test for consensus in the small groups.

13. In the large group, the revised proposal is read again.

14. A test for consensus is held in the entire group.

a mutually satisfactory solution without requiring the entire group to spend time on the potentially arduous process.

## THE "CONSENSUS-TRUST" CONVENTION MODEL

The feminist movement is developing an alternative to Robert's Rules of Order for large meetings where parliamentary procedure would traditionally be used. The "Consensus-Trust" model was first tested successfully at the founding convention of the National Women's Studies Association in 1977, which over 700 people attended. It was modified and used by a smaller group of about 50 at the first Wisconsin State Convention of the National Lesbian Feminist Organization in 1978.

The model is used at meetings whose purpose is to pass resolutions that will stand as policies or platforms for the organization. Resolutions or proposals are drafted prior to the session by small groups. The goal of the meeting is to reach agreement about these proposals where possible, rather than to debate hot issues.

In the "Consensus-Trust" model, participants attempt to reach consensus up to a point, then opt for a two-thirds majority vote in a way that still takes into account the concerns of those who do not support the resolution. (See the accompanying diagram.)

The model uses many techniques already discussed in this chapter. A minute of silence after hearing the resolution gives everyone an opportunity to think about it before speaking. Discussion consists of requesting information for clarification and voicing concerns, rather than a pro-con debate. Ideas emerge in a positive, constructive atmosphere. The group works together to make changes consistent with the intent of the original resolution, but amending, clarifying, or otherwise modifying it to meet concerns expressed.

A vote is taken even when the test for consensus is positive, both for the

ritual value of affirming the agreement and because some people really want the chance to say "yes" to a proposal, rather than just not saying "no."

On a lopsided vote, with two-thirds or more in favor, a caucus meets trying to modify the resolution so it will be more acceptable to the whole group. The revised resolution then either passes with consensus or passes with a two-thirds or more majority. In the latter case, the unmet concerns and the percent of support are recorded as part of the passed resolution. Thus, the value of all participants' opinions is demonstrated.

In the cases of close votes, with less than two-thirds in favor, a hand vote is immediately taken to decide if the group wants to spend more time on it now. At this writing, this part of the process is yet untested, so modifications may emerge as it is practiced and developed. The emphasis here, though, is to use group time to productive ends, not for endless debate on divisive issues. This kind of approach is appropriate for convention meetings where time is short.

The "Consensus-Trust" model uses a team of facilitators, each with specialized jobs. Two facilitators take turns in the active and consulting roles, running the meeting and making procedural decisions, calling for votes, and so forth. A watcher keeps track of items that need to be picked up again later and also consults on procedural decisions. Two notetakers share the job of recording resolutions; a timekeeper clocks and enforces time limits on individual speakers and on parts of the process; and two people on the convention floor pass out papers, count votes, and answer participants' questions or concerns.

Experiences in using this model have been rewarding, even for people who consider themselves jaded as far as meetings go. Participants have reported that the process engenders a humane, cooperative, and creative atmosphere, and that it is workable and flexible. The model represents one attempt to adapt the values

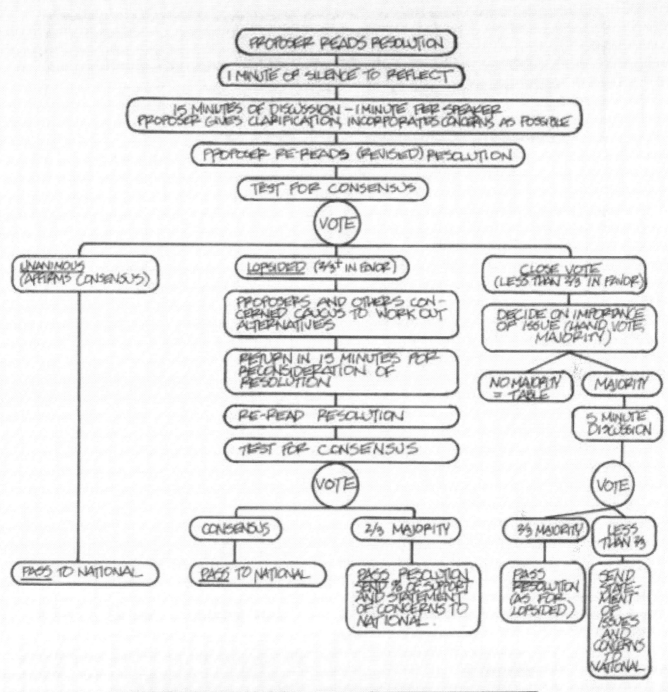

PROPOSER READS RESOLUTION

1 MINUTE OF SILENCE TO REFLECT

15 MINUTES OF DISCUSSION — 1 MINUTE PER SPEAKER
PROPOSER GIVES CLARIFICATION, INCORPORATES CONCERNS AS POSSIBLE

PROPOSER RE-READS (REVISED) RESOLUTION

TEST FOR CONSENSUS

VOTE

UNANIMOUS (AFFIRMS CONSENSUS)

LOPSIDED (2/3+ IN FAVOR)

CLOSE VOTE (LESS THAN 2/3 IN FAVOR)

PROPOSERS AND OTHERS CONCERNED CAUCUS TO WORK OUT ALTERNATIVES

DECIDE ON IMPORTANCE OF ISSUE (HAND VOTE MAJORITY)

RETURN IN 15 MINUTES FOR RECONSIDERATION OF RESOLUTION

NO MAJORITY = TABLE

MAJORITY

RE-READ RESOLUTION

5 MINUTE DISCUSSION

TEST FOR CONSENSUS

VOTE

VOTE

CONSENSUS

2/3 MAJORITY

2/3 MAJORITY

LESS THAN 2/3

PASS TO NATIONAL

PASS TO NATIONAL

PASS RESOLUTION SEND % OF SUPPORT AND STATEMENT OF CONCERNS TO NATIONAL.

PASS RESOLUTION (AS FOR LOPSIDED)

SEND STATEMENT OF ISSUES AND CONCERNS TO NATIONAL

CONSENSUS - TRUST CONVENTION MODEL

105

p 53 – Cely, I disagree if you so many kinds of groups are geographically dispersed and can come together for only 1 or 2 days at a time then the people need other kinds of contact – learning and sharing in workshops, eating and dancing together, etc etc – besides large group decision making meeting. People often won't even _come_ to a gathering if it's all one kind of business. We need to humanize the convention format and help it work for us, with and within all the constraints of that ugly real world where people live and work

and techniques of consensus decision making to the specialized setting of a large group with short time and a product to complete.

A final point: as groups try to adapt the benefits of consensus decision making to situations like conferences and conventions, it is easy to assume that they must work within the traditional frameworks of such situations. Thus people work at changing the decision-making procedures rather than trying to change the situation itself. It might be valuable to experiment with allocating more time for decision making at conferences, or looking for other structural changes that would allow use of something closer to a "straight consensus" process.

### CONCLUSION

The alternatives in this chapter may help you adapt the principles of consensus to a situation where "pure" consensus would not be acceptable or effective. If the specific techniques here do not meet your needs, they may suggest new procedures that your group can develop for its own purposes. We want to caution you, however, that the time to agree on a procedure is before you begin your decision-

making work. Do not try to leap to a new contract about how decisions will be made halfway through a meeting or difficult discussion. Deciding on a process is an important, and sometimes difficult, decision in its own right. It needs to be done separately from group work. Members also need to know the "rules" and to be able to trust that the process will be stable, that it won't change when the going gets hard, and that other members won't try to alter the rules to get their way. If you do need to change your process, set up a time to discuss the changes that is clearly separate from other concerns and decisions you must deal with.

### MOST HIGHLY RECOMMENDED RESOURCES

*RESOURCE MANUAL FOR A LIVING REVOLUTION* (especially section entitled, *"Decision-Making Tools,"* pp. 80-83) by Virginia Coover, et al.

*GROUP TECHNIQUES FOR PROGRAM PLANNING* by Andre Delbecq, et al.

# Chapter 13

# Common Problems: What To Do About Them

Rarely is a meeting perfect. Rarely is the process completely smooth, participation absolutely equal, all conflicts worked through creatively and lovingly, and all decisions inspirationally innovative and entirely satisfactory to everyone. The perfect meeting is, to meeting-goers, as legendary as the perfect wave is to surfers, or the perfect souffle to epicures.

In truth, the best of meetings is usually riddled with small problems: a priority set six months ago with full agreement of the group comes up again as the subject of heated controversy; a group member is in a bad mood and has something negative to say about every proposal. In a good meeting, the members are alert to these small problems and deal with them as they come up, working at the process of the meeting rather than expecting it to run itself.

But occasionally some problem will crop up again and again and will cause much frustration. In order to help your own thinking, we will summarize what we have said in other chapters by addressing common problems that we have encountered in our own group experience. For each of these problems, we will outline the symptoms, possible causes of those symptoms, and what you might do about them.

Our approach will consist mainly of referencing previous chapters and telling you where to seek further information, rather than reviewing subjects discussed elsewhere. Of course this list cannot be complete. Each group is unique in its own way, and these suggestions should be adapted to the needs of your particular group.

## I. POLARIZED FACTIONS

### The Symptoms

The members of your group seem to break up into two or more small factions that repeatedly disagree with one another on a variety of issues. This disagreement has occurred consistently enough that the members of the factions expect to disagree with each other and are more conscious of their areas of disagreement than of any agreement they share. They resent each other and this increases polarization.

### The Analysis and What To Do

One or both of the underlying problems described below could be causing these factions.

## A. There is a Real, Philosophical Split in the Group

Analysis: For a group to work well, members should be aware of commonly held agreement on purpose, goals, or expectations. During times of stress, it helps to remind a group of what they share in common, despite their differences. Yet even when a group does share a common goal, individuals may have different beliefs about the best way of achieving that goal. Or they may have different beliefs about the priorities of their goals.

What To Do: When differences in underlying philosophy or perspective cause repeated disagreements over similar topics, it is time to discuss these topics in depth. You might hold a priorities-setting meeting, a goals-identification meeting, or a retreat where members discuss why the group is important to them, what they value about their experience together, what their frustrations are, what changes they would like to see. Try to balance the discussion of theoretical issues with practical concerns. Having a facilitator or consultant from outside the group may help since he or she will not be personally involved in the group's conflicts. *See Chapter 10, CONFLICT AND PROBLEM SOLVING.*

## B. There is A Long-Term Unresolved Conflict

Analysis: This conflict doesn't have to be about philosophical issues, as described above, but it may have the same effect of splitting the group.

Example: Several members, at a previous meeting, objected to the group's policy of allowing John to make independent financial decisions, and a subcommittee was formed to make such decisions in the future. Now John feels angry about the lack of trust shown towards him and about his own loss of freedom. Several others also feel that he was treated unfairly and support him when he dissents about

**MITOSIS: CREATIVE GROUP DIVISION**

"One of my absolute beliefs is that any movement which has been based on freedom . . . is like a live cell; there is a biology of ideas as there is a biology of cells, and each goes through a process of evolution. The parent cell splits and the new entities in their turn divide and divide again. Instead of indicating a breakdown, it is a sign of health; endless energy is spent trying to keep together forces which should be distinct. Each cell is fulfilling its mission in this separation, which in point of fact is no separation at all. Cohesion is maintained until in the end the whole is a vast mosaic cleaving together in union and strength.

--from Margaret Sanger
*AN AUTOBIOGRAPHY*
W. W. Norton and Company
New York, 1938  pp. 396-7

other matters. The individuals who had requested the change in policy sense John's resentment and are on the defensive when he disagrees with them. As a result, factions develop around issues that are completely unrelated to the original conflict.

What To Do: It is important to bring such underlying conflicts into the open and deal with them. Sometimes members will act under the influence of such conflicts without realizing it. If you suspect an underlying conflict is disrupting your group, bring it up for group discussion. Pick a time to ask: "What's really going on here?" Initially, members may be unwilling to admit that they still hold resentments about something that is supposed to be "dead and buried" (or that was never openly acknowledged in the first place). If the group tries to work things out in a supportive atmosphere, rather than laying blame or making accusations, individuals can often recognize and address the problem, or at least discharge some of the tension. If the factionalism has been intense, your group may need some trust building exercises before things can be dealt with openly. *See: Chapter 10, CONFLICT AND PROBLEM SOLVING, and "Increase Involvement and Trust" in Chapter 11, TECHNIQUES FOR GROUP BUILDING. You may also want to review Chapter 9, WORKING WITH EMOTIONS.*

## II.  ENDLESS DISCUSSION

### The Symptoms

Simple decisions sometimes turn into long, heated debates.  For more complex decisions, discussion can go on and on and never seem to get anywhere.

### The Analysis and What To Do

The root of this symptom may be one of the problems described above under *"Polarized Factions."*  Read that section as well as examining the thoughts below.

A.  Members Are Competitive, Too Strongly Identified With Their Own Ideas, or Afraid to Trust One Another

Analysis:  Consensus requires an atmosphere of cooperation and support. Members must feel they can trust each other, they must care about each other's needs, and they must avoid competitive attempts to "win" a decision-making "contest."  *See Chapter 3, ATTITUDES AND CONSENSUS, and Chapter 4, YOUR PARTICIPATION IN THE CONSENSUS PROCESS.*

Believing in such values, however, is much easier than acting on them.  Even in groups which encourage members to act in open, trusting ways, and to express their feelings, "false trust" is often a problem.  Individuals may act trusting because they feel pressured to do so in order to be accepted, but deep down the feeling of trust isn't there yet.  Try to recognize in yourself the difference between making an effort to be a little more open and trusting and the mere mimicry of such attitudes.

What To Do:  Recognize that it is a struggle always to feel cooperative, always to avoid attachment to your own ideas, and always to trust others to listen and care.  Members can help one another when changes in attitude and behavior are sought.

Example:  Laura has something argumentative to say every time someone expresses an opinion that is substantially different from hers.  It is right for people to criticize this behavior and to gently pressure her to act differently.  But at the same time, the group can help by recognizing why she is acting this way.  Is it because the decision is personally important to her and she is afraid people will forget to consider the points she has raised?  If so, others can assure her that they have heard her and will remember to consider her points (then they really will make a special effort to do so).  When Jack states a counter argument, he can say: "I think the point Laura just raised is important to to be kept in mind. I think we should also consider the other side of the coin, which is . . ."

Group evaluations are good tools for helping members in the never-ending struggle to be good contributors.  During evaluations members can make a special effort to recognize participation problems, to offer and to ask for help.  *See "Evaluations" in Chapter 6, STRUCTURING YOUR MEETINGS, and "Feedback and Criticism," in Chapter 8, COMMUNICATION SKILLS.*

The group can also work on building a more cohesive and supportive group climate where people will feel safer about trusting each other.  *See Chapter 11, TECHNIQUES FOR GROUP BUILDING.  Also look at Chapter 9, WORKING WITH EMOTIONS, for ideas about what to do "along the way." -- We are always along the way.*

**109**

## B. The Subject Itself Is Too Unwieldy

**Analysis:** Does everyone know exactly what decisions you are trying to make? Was the goal of the discussion clear at the beginning, but new issues have arisen and clouded your purpose? Is the subject too vague or complicated?

**What To Do:** You need a more structured agenda for organizing your approach to the problem. Perhaps the issue should be broken into smaller parts which can be discussed separately. Perhaps it can be "pre-digested" so part of the thinking is done before the meeting. *See "Working Outside of the Meeting" in Chapter 6, STRUCTURING YOUR MEETINGS. Also review the techniques of clarifying and reformulating described in "Facilitative Functions" in Chapter 7, THE ROLE OF THE GROUP FACILITATOR.*

## C. Group Members Have "Hidden Agendas"

**Analysis:** The issue that is being discussed is not the real, or the only, issue under consideration.

**Example:** The group is supposedly deciding <u>which</u> project to undertake next, but an unstated issue, perhaps important to many people, perhaps just to one or two, is <u>whose</u> project will be worked on. In other words, a power struggle is happening.

**Example:** David is arguing against a particular expenditure because he wants the money to remain available for a different purchase, one he hasn't proposed yet.

Unrecognized hidden agendas can cause discussion to flounder hopelessly. The group can't come to agreement since the issues being addressed aren't the only ones influencing people.

**What To Do:** What the group needs is more clarity about the real issues at hand. Usually if one person can identify the underlying issue, an "aha!" response in the group will be followed by relief that the real issue is out in the open. Many times participants don't realize they are being influenced by a hidden agenda. It may take a group effort to stop and ask, "What is really going on here? Everybody look inward for a moment, please."

**110**

Don't be accusatory in pointing out another person's hidden agenda. Act in a cooperative effort to achieve clarity. If you suddenly realize that you have been under the influence of a hidden agenda yourself, point it out to the group. Doing this will not only explain your motivations to them but might also stimulate a new perspective in others. Hidden agendas are more successfully exposed and dealt with when the group's norms encourage discussion of process and feelings. *Review Chapter 4, YOUR PARTICIPATION IN THE CONSENSUS PROCESS, Chapter 9, WORKING WITH EMOTIONS, and Chapter 11, TECHNIQUES FOR GROUP BUILDING.*

### D. Discussion Meanders Because of Poor Facilitation.

Analysis: Constant attention is required to keep a group focused on a single topic of discussion and to maintain a clear understanding of where the discussion is moving. One person usually takes responsibility for this task, but the more members skilled in facilitation, the better the process will be.

What To Do: Emphasize learning and using facilitation skills by the whole group. Discuss facilitation when you evaluate your meetings. *See "Evaluations" in Chapter 6, STRUCTURING YOUR MEETINGS, and see Chapter 7, THE ROLE OF THE GROUP FACILITATOR.*

### III. LOW QUALITY DECISIONS

## The Symptoms

Your group agrees to a decision, but finds out later that many people are actually dissatisfied with the decision and are not committed to carrying it out. Or perhaps a decision originally seemed good, but later it becomes apparent that it is inadequate: it won't work; it doesn't meet some important needs; or everyone originally thought they knew what the decision was, but now several people have different memories of what the agreement actually meant.

## The Analysis and What To Do

Poor decisions may result from unwieldly discussions or poor facilitation, addressed above under Sections II.B. and II.D. If neither of these rings a bell, the answer may be below.

### A. The Decision Was Made On Insufficient Information.

Analysis: Probably not enough groundwork was done in advance of the actual decision-making discussion, not enough time was spent exchanging the information that was available, or not enough questions were asked at the time the decision was being made.

What To Do: If your group realizes that it doesn't have enough information, it is best to delay making a decision while more facts and ideas are sought. If you are under urgent time pressure, you might set a special meeting, delegate a subgroup representing different viewpoints to get the information and make a decision, or mandate someone to find out the answers and go ahead on the basis of those answers (e.g., if it costs more than $45 to repair the ditto machine then get rid of it. If it costs less, borrow a truck and take it to the repair shop.) *See "Working Outside of Meetings" in Chapter 6, STRUCTURING YOUR MEETINGS.*

### B. Your Decisions Are Incomplete

Analysis: You aren't rounding decisions out with details about implementation and accountability, or you aren't recording your decisions for later reference. It seems like a decision gets made, but then nothing happens.

What To Do: Be specific. You need to decide how a decision will be carried out, when, by whom, and with what kind of follow-up. *See the box on "The Recorder's Responsibilities," and the section titled "Recording and Implementing Decisions" in Chapter 6, STRUCTURING YOUR MEETING.*

**111**

C. Decisions Are Passed, Despite Underlying Disagreements, Because Members Fear Conflict

Analysis: Members should not feel they have to avoid conflict. Conflict is an important part of the consensus process and a skilled group should be able to survive and grow from the experience.

What To Do: *See Chapter 10, CONFLICT AND PROBLEM SOLVING, for guidelines about dealing with conflict, and Chapter 8, COMMUNICATION SKILLS, for useful skills to use during conflict. See Chapter 11, TECHNIQUES FOR GROUP BUILDING, especially the section titled "Increase Involvement and Trust" for ways of improving intra-group relations and providing the solidarity needed for members to know their group can survive conflict. If you want still more, some useful techniques for coping with potentially frightening situations can be found in Chapter 9, WORKING WITH EMOTIONS.*

D. Time Pressure Is Causing You To Rush Through Decision Making Too Quickly.

Analysis: Occasionally time pressure causes real, inescapable problems. Usually, though, time pressure can be avoided.

What To Do. There are two kinds of time pressure. General pressure occurs when your group just has too much to do in too little meeting time. All decisions get rushed. In this case, consider whether some decisions could be delegated, instead of taking up the time of the whole group. With issues that do demand the whole group's attention, try to organize discussion so its focus is clear and members can address issues directly and efficiently. *See: "Using Agendas" and "Working Outside of Meetings" in Chapter 6, STRUCTURING YOUR MEETING; Chapter 7, THE ROLE OF THE GROUP FACILI-*

THINGS WE NEED TO BE DOING
THAT WE FREQUENTLY DON'T DO

1. Assure that all people can feel comfortable as part of the group, by going slowly to leave room for quieter people, and by showing support for people.

2. Taking time to make sure we understand what is going on.

3. Listening to others carefully; saying when we do not understand what they have said.

4. Building on what others say; synthesizing, rather than putting ideas in conflict.

5. Thinking creatively—breaking out of ruts, looking for new alternatives.

6. Spending time preparing for meetings—arranging thoughts coherently in advance.

7. Building understanding of, and skills in using, the consensus process.

from INVERT

*TATOR; and "Formalized Process" in Chapter 12, ADAPTATIONS OF THE PROCESS FOR SPECIAL SITUATIONS.*

When a particular decision must be made quickly, a group faces a second kind of time pressure. (For example, you must decide whether to publically endorse a particular candidate at a rally tomorrow night.) Sometimes these pressures create a real crisis and there's not much to do except the best you can under the circumstances. On the other hand, groups often perceive themselves to be at the mercy of time pressures that actually can be changed.

Ask yourselves whether such a change is possible in this case. If it really is not, and if the group is having a hard time agreeing, it is probably best not to force a decision. Consider what the

112

costs of not deciding will be. (Will the candidate lose the election without your support? Will your support be just as useful if it comes two weeks later?) Weigh these factors before you rush through a decision.

If you find yourselves repeatedly encountering similar urgent deadlines, you may want to form a policy or develop a contingency plan for making certain kinds of decisions. *Your group may want to review Chapter 5, WHEN AGREEMENT CANNOT BE REACHED, as well as the references mentioned already for this situation.*

E. Decisions Are Poor Because of Incomplete Participation By Group Members

Analysis: Your decision does not represent the active sharing of ideas by all group members.

What To Do: This problem is addressed in the section below on nonparticipation.

IV. NONPARTICIPATION BY SOME MEMBERS

The Symptoms

Some members sit quietly through meetings and don't participate much. More active members may fail to notice this lack of involvement, or they may be disturbed by it. They feel out of touch with the quiet members, don't know what they are thinking, or whether they support the group's activity or not.

Analysis and What To Do

While perfect equality of participation is an ideal that goes hand-in-hand with equality of power in a group, a complete balance of participation is never achieved. Straining too hard for it may disrupt the natural balance of interchange in your group. When individuals do not express themselves in group discussions, however, whether through lack of desire, inability, or by being overpowered by other group members, the whole group suffers.

A. Low Participation Is a Personal Characteristic of These Members

Analysis: Silent members are shy, lack necessary communication skills, or simply have a reticent style of participation.

What To Do: These members may need special support from the group, or acceptance as they are. The rest of the group needs to understand their reasons for being silent. *These issues are addressed in Chapter 11, TECHNIQUES FOR GROUP BUILDING, under the section "Share Responsibility."*

B. Group Members Are "Burning Out"

Analysis: The group has spent its quota of emotional and physical energy and can't continue with efficiency or enthusiasm.

cion.
Should burnout be at least paraphrased, if not defined?
Group members are "burning out."

Sea. Someone else also thinks "burn out" is not a fully-accredited word. I personally do not think it will be around in 10 years. -Brian

s: The group has spent its quota of emotional and physical energy and can't

farther efficiently or enthusiastically.

The burn-out may arise out of this particular meeting. It has lasted

What To Do: The "burn-out" may arise out of this particular meeting: it has lasted too long, has been too boring, or too emotionally intense, or it comes at the end of an arduous week. Take a break, change the subject, do a "light and lively" exercise, or reschedule the meeting for another time and go out for pizza. *See Chapter 9, WORKING WITH EMOTIONS, and Chapter 11, TECHNIQUES FOR GROUP BUILDING.*

On the other hand, the burn-out may be a long-term problem. At such times it's crucial to re-examine the group, the way it works, and what it is doing to find out what the problem is. Are your activities unrewarding? Are your meetings too drawn out and tiring? If the group is taking energy away from its members, and if members aren't being recharged somehow (by cameraderie with other members, by a dedication to a purpose, by feelings of success, or by a balance of rewarding, challenging tasks against the tedious ones), then something needs to be changed or disaster will occur. It's time to do some concentrated evaluating and possibly to change goals or procedures. *See Chapter 6, STRUCTURING YOUR MEETINGS, for suggestions about doing evaluations and for ideas about streamlining your meeting process. Also see the references mentioned in the paragraph above.*

### C. Silent Members Lack Trust In The Group or Fear Conflict

Analysis: Individuals do not speak their minds because they fear speaking will bring undesirable consequences. They think other members may launch a critical attack on the statement, someone's feelings will be hurt by disagreement, or an ugly conflict will ensue.

What To Do: If your group fosters norms of trust and caring, and if conflict is accepted as natural, then this fear of putting oneself on the line (which everyone experiences to some degree) shouldn't keep members from saying what they feel is important. *Again, see Chapter 11,*

*TECHNIQUES FOR GROUP BUILDING, on fostering supportive norms in a group. Look at Chapter 8, COMMUNICATION SKILLS, Chapter 10, CONFLICT AND PROBLEM SOLVING, and Chapter 9, WORKING WITH EMOTIONS, for specific skills that make these norms work.*

### D. A Member is Reticent Because of Lack of Commitment

Analysis: The individual just isn't interested, or doesn't care anymore what the group does or decides.

What To Do: The group needs an explanation of this feeling. Is it because the member is no longer very interested in the group? Does he or she have needs that aren't being met? Are there particular frustrations with the role the member plays? Does he or she feel left out, ignored, unchallenged? Or is it a natural growing away from the group as interests change? If these conditions are long term, they may signal a need for change. The person may need to assume a different role in the group, address problems in relationships with group members, or possibly leave the group. This may be a private decision, but the group should be informed so it knows what to expect and understands why the member is choosing to alter his or her relationship with the group. In other cases, the needed change may affect other people, or the member may need to share and receive input from the group. A special time can be set aside for discussing these concerns.

If the lack of commitment or interest applies just to the particular project or item being dealt with at the moment, the group may tolerate a member's not participating in the discussion at hand. Or they may believe that the issue is of basic importance to the group and they will ask the particular member, as part of his or her commitment to the group as a whole, to take part in this matter despite personal lack of interest.

Finally, a member may fade away from the group due to individual burn-out. He or

she is overextended in activities and
commitments, or a personal crisis (e.g.,
illness, a problem at home) is using up
energy. Burn-out is a special problem
in consensus groups since they require
such a high level of involvement from
all members. Many times members make
demands on each other's energy just when
they should instead remind one another
to take care of themselves and to treat
their energy as a limited and valued resource. Group members need a balance between working together for the good of
the whole group and nurturing the individuals in the group. If they let
each other pay too high a price for the
group's sake, more will be lost than
gained. If a person is truly burned out,
she or he needs group support. It is OK
to take a leave of absence, to cut back
time involvement by doing less, or to cut
back emotional involvement (perhaps by
doing only clerical work for a while instead of stressful planning or negotiat-
ing activities). If a member doesn't get
this kind of support from the group when
he or she is burning out, the final result may be the person's giving up and
withdrawing completely, or leaving in
anger and bitterness. *See Chapter 9,
WORKING WITH EMOTIONS, and Chapter 11,
TECHNIQUES FOR GROUP BUILDING.*

[Beware] of the tendency
to see consensus decision
making as the process
that good, nice people
use — ie, a good in
itself, regardless of
context.
                    —Trudy Cooper

## V. SOME INDIVIDUALS DOMINATE DISCUSSION

### The Symptoms

One or a few members speak the most at
meetings. Perhaps this over-participation is recognized by the group as a
problem and is a source of frustration.
Or perhaps it is generally accepted because these people also have disproportionate power in the group. Either way,
it will interfere with the consensus process.

### Analysis and What To Do

Over-participation may reflect a power
imbalance, or it may be the result of
other factors in an individual's participation style.

#### A. There Is a Power Imbalance

Analysis: The members who speak most
have the most control over what the group
does. Other members, whether they like
the situation or not, find themselves de-
ferring to these people.

What To Do: Sometimes members get
satisfaction out of having excessive power in a group. Often, though, they would
like to get out of that role and have
other members share the burden of responsibility. (In workshops we have done,
there are usually as many people asking
"How do I give up the power I have?" as
there are ones who want to know, "How
do I get more power?") Whichever the
situation in your group, the best approach is to openly acknowledge the problem and work together to change it. This
change will be most effective if it is
attempted cooperatively rather than as a
coup against the "establishment." Remember the scope for defensiveness that exists when someone's power is challenged.
Even when a person would like to hand over
some responsibility, it is often difficult to see a less experienced person do
something differently than you would yourself, and perhaps make mistakes. It is
also scarey to take on new responsibilities. Often power imbalances continue

to exist, with resentments on both sides, because members are afraid, or don't know how, to instigate change. If treated as a mutual struggle, without laying blame on individuals for their mistakes or their roles, the move towards more equal participation can be a rewarding learning experience for everyone. *See "Share Responsibility" in Chapter 11, TECHNIQUES FOR GROUP BUILDING, for specific hints about equalizing involvement. See "Feedback and Criticism" in Chapter 8, COMMUNICATION SKILLS, for tools that can be used in talking about the situation. Finally, see Chapter 9, WORKING WITH EMOTIONS, and Chapter 10, CONFLICT AND PROBLEM SOLVING, for guidelines about working with the feelings and conflicts involved.*

## B. Individuals Just Talk Too Much At Meetings

Analysis: This volubility reflects some characteristic in the member's style other than power in the group.

What To Do: Try to find out why the person talks so much. Maybe he or she likes being in the limelight. More likely he or she lacks confidence. Sometimes people drone on about a subject because they are afraid that others won't hear and understand what they have to say, or that if they don't have a comeback for every objection, others will forget the important points they have raised. Using the communications skills *(described under "Feedback and Criticism" in Chapter 8, COMMUNICATION SKILLS)* explain to the person how he or she is causing a problem in the group and what specific changes you would like to see. If the group climate is supportive, and if the person can recognize the validity of the need for a change in speaking style, then the whole group can support this change. During meetings, members can: a) assure the over-participating person that he or she is being heard; and b) point out when the person slips back into the problem behavior ("Paula, can you get to the point more quickly please?" -- "Are you going to say something different that

you haven't already said before?"). This is a good time for humor (or at least good humor) that lets the individual know he or she is accepted by the group, despite the fact that the group isn't tolerating a specific behavior. The more that blame and accusation can be avoided, the better. But do be direct.

Good facilitation skills can help a member be aware of the need for equalizing participation, for staying on the topic and being relevant in all remarks, and for being aware of the progress of a discussion and the whole group's needs. You might have the monopolizer share facilitation with another, skilled facilitator. This can increase the person's sensitivity to his or her own speaking style. *(See Chapter 7, THE ROLE OF THE GROUP FACILITATOR; also see Section II.A. above under "Endless Discussion.")*

## VI. A GROUP MEMBER APPARENTLY WON'T COOPERATE

### The Symptom

A group member seems to be totally uncooperative despite considerable effort on improving skills and sharing responsibility. Such a member may be disrupting the whole group's ability to work effectively.

### Analysis and What To Do

When such situations occur they are painful, bewildering and frustrating for all concerned. We don't have any smooth solutions to fall back on. *(For an "ideal" resolution to such a problem, see the boxed example, "A Case Study of Problem Solving," in Chapter 10, CONFLICT AND PROBLEM SOLVING.)* However, you should be sure that the group is justified in considering that a true case of non-cooperation exists, and that the group is not merely scapegoating someone who has a legitimate but different perspective on important issues.

**116**

A. The "Non-Cooperation" of a Member
May Be Resolved Into a Set of
Strong Disagreements Which Can
Be Solved or at Least Mutually
Acknowledged

Analysis: Sometimes a member who is causing considerable disruption in a group is labeled as "uncooperative" because the status quo is being shaken or because cherished assumptions are being questioned. Often the person may have good intentions but poor communication skills.

What To Do:

--a) Deal with problems caused by a member's behavior as early as possible. When people are committed to "cooperating" and to "accepting differences," it is often very hard to express anger toward another person whose views or behaviors are different. Often each member will sit back waiting for someone else to be the first to complain. This only allows time for anger to grow and for everyone to build a more solid "case" against the problem member. When stored anger finally erupts, the member can be scapegoated by the rest of the group, and the situation is almost always made worse. The problem member feels alone and alienated, whether he or she recognizes the source of this feeling or not; and other members begin reinforcing each other's anger and blame. It is hard to think rationally when this happens. So speak up soon, even about little things, while you're still willing and able to do it in a supportive, give-and-take manner. *(See "Guidelines for Responding to Conflict" in Chapter 10, CONFLICT AND PROBLEM SOLVING. See "Feedback and Criticism" in Chapter 8, COMMUNICATION SKILLS.)*

--b) Assume for as long as you can that the person wants to cooperate and offer whatever help you can to make this possible.

A new, probationary, member of a primarily volunteer group had asked for employment in the group's office during the summer. It was decided that he should have an evaluation session, to see if the group wanted to accept him as a full member, before his employment was considered. During the evaluation session many members expressed great anger and frustration at his behavior in the group. Serious problems were pointed out about his participation in meetings. However, after the anger was vented, the group decided to delay the decision about whether he could be a full member of the group, but to go ahead and give him the summer job. During the period of his employment, he had a better chance to learn about the group and its members, and people were able to get to know him better. He began to fit in. In the fall, the group was happy to accept him as a regular member.

--c) Listen to the problem member. What are his or her perceptions of the situation? Try to identify with that perspective. *(See "Listening" in Chapter 8, COMMUNICATION SKILLS.)*

--d) Question your own analysis. Is it a case of absolute non-cooperation, or is it just easier for you to dismiss a person who works and thinks differently from the rest of the group?

--e) Consider third pary mediation. In cases of protracted and strong disagreement, a person outside the group may see the issue more clearly than anyone in the group can hope to. *(See "Problem Solving" in Chapter 10, CONFLICT AND PROBLEM SOLVING.)*

--f) As a last resort, you might want to try changing the person's role in the group or asking the person to take a leave of absence while everyone cools off.

**117**

## B. The Member Is Truly Non-Cooperative

Analysis: If every effort toward pinpointing and resolving differences between a member and the group have failed, then you may be justified in thinking of a member as non-cooperative. It is crucial to realize that such a label has little to say about the true causes of the situation. People are, after all, not uncooperative out of sheer diabolical intent. They have reasons which, however convoluted to others, make sense to them. A person may be acting out of personal needs (e.g. for more attention or greater influence), or perhaps he or she wishes to make the group over in an image which no one in the group can comprehend, let alone agree to or act on. Or perhaps mutual antagonism has reached a destructive phase that cannot be controlled.

What To Do: There is little point in trying to completely uncover the reasons for uncooperativeness. But it is still important to recognize that such an explanation does exist, even when the only solution is to ask the problem member to leave the group. This awareness makes it possible to offer the person sympathetic respect for his or her feelings during the process of separation and it lessens the sense of failure and the desire for recriminations on both sides. Use the occasion to do some serious evaluating of your group's process (perhaps with input from the problem member), to think about things you can change for the better, and to do some group building activities to help you feel good about yourselves again. *(See "Evaluations" in Chapter 6, STRUCTURING YOUR MEETINGS, Chapter 9, WORKING WITH EMOTIONS, and Chapter 11, TECHNIQUES FOR GROUP BUILDING.)*

### AUTHORS' NOTE

This section on non-cooperating members was added as an afterthought near the end of our writing process. We realized we had avoided addressing this thorny problem by a neat trick of reasoning: consensus presupposes cooperation, so if someone is not cooperating, it is not consensus; ergo, we don't have to talk about it.

If only.

Finally we forced ourselves to face facts and admitted that this is one of the situations that consensus groups sometimes face. Fortunately it happens only rarely. But once in a lifetime is enough.

So we put ourselves on the line and said the best we could on the subject. We don't mean to imply by our step-by-step "recipe" that you can face such a problem easily, methodically and painlessly. It is almost always messy and confusing and unpleasant.

Go forth bravely, friends. Mistakes will be made, but you can only do your best and learn from the process. If there is a silver lining here, it's the fact that surviving such times almost always results in groups and individuals learning better skills and gaining understanding that can help in the future.

--Chel

# Bibliography

Below are some publications that we have found useful for understanding consensus groups and how they work. We have tried to be selective, rather than comprehensive, in the materials we included here, and to let you know why we chose each title. Some come with wholehearted recommendations, some with qualified recommendations: our annotations will make the differentiation for you.

Some of these materials are produced by small or private presses and must be mail ordered. We have given you all the information we have about how to acquire such publications, including the last known price. Since printing and postage rates vary rapidly, you may want to double check with a source before making an order.

Auvine, Brian, Betsy Densmore, Mary Extrom, Scott Poole and Michel Shanklin, *A MANUAL FOR GROUP FACILITATORS*, 1977. The Center for Conflict Resolution (731 State Street, Madison, WI 53703, $4.50 + $1.10 postage). The values, assumptions and techniques of group facilitation. Especially useful to people planning workshops. Includes sections on communication, conflict, problem solving, what can go wrong and what to do about it, and many other relevant topics.

Bartoo, Glenn, *DECISIONS BY CONSENSUS: A STUDY OF THE QUAKER METHOD*, 1978. Progressive Publisher (401 E. 32nd, No. 1002, Chicago, IL 60616, $1). Condensed from a 1952 thesis describing consensus as practiced by the 57th St. Friends Meeting of Chicago. Describes how consensus operates and what makes it work.

Becker, Norma, *"Beyond the Abdication of Power," in WIN*, Dec. 7, 1978. (326 Livingston, Brooklyn, N.Y. 11217, 212/624-8337.) Presents an argument against the views expressed by Kokopeli and Lakey in *LEADERSHIP FOR CHANGE*. We include it for the thought-provoking issues it raises and because it demonstrates situations and assumptions under which consensus is not appropriate.

Bookchin, Murray. *POST SCARCITY ANARCH-ISM*, 1971. Ramparts Press, San Francisco. A collection of essays presenting an alternate vision of power through analysis of the ways people work together and the goals people choose.

Case, John and Rosemary Talor, eds., *CO-OPS, COMMUNES AND COLLECTIVES: EXPERIMENTS IN SOCIAL CHANGE IN THE 1960'S AND 1970'S*, 1979. Pantheon Books, N.Y. Contains case studies of alternative organisations and articles addressing issues relevant to how such organizations function. Particularly good is Jane J. Mansbridge's paper, *"The Agony of Inequality."* Also recommended: *"Conditions for Democracy: Making Participatory Organizations Work"* by Joyce Rothschild-Whitt.

Coover, Virginia, Ellen Deacon, Charles Esser and Christopher Moore, *RESOURCE MANUAL FOR A LIVING REVOLUTION*, 1977. Movement for a New Society (4722 Baltimore Ave., Philadelphia, PA 19143, $5). An excellent presentation of the personal, interpersonal and group skills necessary for nonviolent social change, as well as the theory and arguments for social change activity.

The sections on working in groups and developing communities of support provide a wealth of valuable information and ideas.

Craig, James H. and Marge, *SYNERGIC POWER: BEYOND DOMINATION AND PERMIS-SIVENESS*, 1973. Proactive Press (Box 296, Berkeley, CA 94701). Suggests tools for generating creative coopera-tion in personal relations and on a social scale. Analyzes human nature, human potential and power dynamics, then offers a model for developing a cooperative, "synergic society."

Delbecq, Andre, Andrew H. Van de Van, and David H. Gustafson, *GROUP TECHNIQUES FOR PROGRAM PLANNING: A GUIDE TO NOM-INAL AND DELPHI PROCESSES*, 1975. Scott, Foresman and Co. Presents two highly adaptable methods for high-involvement decision making in large groups. Some of the more "progressive" work coming out of business schools in the 1970's.

Filley, Alan, *INTERPERSONAL CONFLICT RESOLUTION*, 1975. Scott, Foresman and Co. (Glenview, IL, $5.95). Exam-ines conflict dynamics, strategies of resolution, and personal styles of responding to conflict. The coopera-tive model for "Integrative Decision Making" is the basis for the Creative Problem Solving technique presented in Chapter 10 of this book. Recom-mended for anyone who wants a more in-depth understanding of this ap-proach. Written from a business man-agement perspective.

Fluegelman, Andrew, ed., *THE NEW GAMES BOOK*, 1976. Dolphin Books/Doubleday and Co., Inc., Garden City, N.Y. A collection of noncompetitive, "play hard" games from the New Games Founda-tion. Emphasis is on fun and coopera-tion. Highly recommended.

French, J.R.P. and B. Raven, *"The Bases of Social Power," in* D. Cartwright, ed., *STUDIES IN SOCIAL POWER*, 1959. University of Michigan, Ann Arbor. A classic, scholarly article analyz-ing the different ways in which people come to exert power or influence over others. Written with formal, hierar-chical organizations in mind, but highly adaptable for understanding small group dynamics.

Freundlich, Paul, Chris Collins and Mikki Wenig, *A GUIDE TO COOPERATIVE ALTERNATIVES*, 1979. Community Publi-cations Cooperative (P.O. Box 426, Louisa, VA 23093. $5.95). Edited by *"Communities, Journal of Coopera-tive Living,"* this book is a resource guide of ideas, resources, references and contacts for people interested in living and working cooperatively. Includes well-annotated sections on politics, decision making, education, community organizing and much more.

Friedman, Anita, *"Mediations,"* 1973. Issues in Radical Therapy Collective (Box 23544, Oakland, CA 94623, 50¢). A step-by-step approach to solving interpersonal conflicts using radical therapy principles and a third-party facilitator. (Also available as a chapter in H. Wyckoff's *LOVE, THERAPY AND POLITICS*.)

Geeting, Baxter and Corinne, *HOW TO LISTEN ASSERTIVELY*, 1976. Monarch, N.Y. A whole book about listening! (Actually, the concepts here could be presented, less cutely, in one, concise chapter.) Emphasizes the importance of attentive, open-minded listening using plenty of metaphors and examples to drive the principles home. Worth reading.

Gordon, Thomas, *PARENT EFFECTIVENESS TRAINING*, 1970. Peter H. Wyden, Inc., N.Y. Describes communication skills that are useful in conflict situations (e.g., "I messages" and "active listen-ing"). Written about conflicts with children, but universally applicable.

Guthrie, Eileen and Sam Miller, *MAKING CHANGE*, 1977. Consultants for Com-munity Development (2535 Columbus Ave., South, Minneapolis, MN, $6). How to effect community change as an indi-vidual or as a member of a support group, a neighborhood organization, a board of directors, or other political group. Organizing skills, conflict diagnosis and resolution, communication skills, and running meetings are a few of the skills described in the context of neighborhood/community change.

Harrison, Marta, *FOR THE FUN OF IT! SELECTED COOPERATIVE GAMES FOR CHILDREN AND ADULTS*, 1975. Nonviolence and Children (Friends Peace Committee, 1515 Cherry St., Philadelphia, PA 19102, $1.25 + 40¢ postage). Activities that groups of adults, kids, or a mixture can use to develop cooperation and to have fun.

Hopkins, Robert, *"Consensus Decision Making: An Analysis of the Literature,"* 1977. Can order from The Center for Conflict Resolution (731 State St., Madison, WI 53703, $3 for copying and postage). Includes a look at historical interest in consensus, an overview of research with critiques, and recommendations for future research. Brings together most of the current empirical findings in research about consensus.

Hopkins, Robert, *"Multivariate Analysis of Two 'Competing' Theories of Consensus Decision Making,"* 1978. Can order from The Center for Conflict Resolution (731 State St., Madison, WI 53703, $3 for copying and postage). Builds on current theories (by J. Hall) to propose steps necessary to ensure maximum quality and acceptance of a consensus decision.

INVERT (Institute for Nonviolence Education, Research and Training, RFD 1, Newport, ME 04953). This organization has developed several inexpensive publications (including *"Consensus Education Packet"* and *"Sharing Consensus: A Handbook for Consensus Workshops"*) which describe how consensus works, how to participate effectively, and how to teach consensus skills. They seem to be continually developing their materials

and replacing them with new and better ones. We encourage you to write them, especially if your group is just beginning to use consensus, and inquire about their latest publications.

Johnson, David and Frank, *JOINING TOGETHER: GROUP THEORY AND GROUP SKILLS*, 1975. Prentice-Hall, Inc., Englewood Cliffs, NJ. A practical learning guide that includes both theory and activities to improve understanding and skills in subjects such as group dynamics, leadership, conflict, communication and group decision making.

Joreen, *"The Tyranny of Structurelessness,"* originally printed in *"Second Wave,"* Vol. II, No. 1. Available from KNOW, Inc. (P.O. Box 86031, Pittsburgh, PA 15221). A sharp analysis and critique of problems in "leaderless" groups in the women's movement. Advocates explicit, agreed-upon norms to regulate power dynamics. A "classic" in the literature of democratic group process.

Kokopeli, Bruce and George Lakey, *"Leadership for Change,"* 1978. Movement for a New Society, (4722 Baltimore Ave., Philadelphia, PA 19143, $1.25). Traditional, "patriarchal" leadership is compared to "feminist" or shared leadership in groups. Tactics for changing leadership style are described.

Lakey, Berit, *"Meeting Facilitation: The No-Magic Method,"* 1975. Movement for a New Society (4722 Baltimore Ave., Philadelphia, PA 19143, 60¢). Short, straight-forward, how-to instructions explain what facilitation is, how to use an agenda, and tips for helping the group along. (Also appears as a chapter in *BUILDING SOCIAL CHANGE COMMUNITIES* by The Training/Action Affinity Group.)

Lyons, Gracie, *CONSTRUCTIVE CRITICISM: A HANDBOOK*, 1976. Issues in Radical Therapy (P.O. Box 5039, Berkeley, CA 94705, $3). The need for, logic behind, and techniques of constructive criticism in groups. Includes detailed description of specific skills. Written for Marxist activists, but useful for anyone.

Machiavelli, Giavonni, *THE PRINCE*, 1952. Mentor Classics, The New American Library. The classic analysis of power and politics (originally published during the Italian Renaissance). It is rare to find such a clear and explicit representation of the traditional approach to political and social control.

*"Ms. Magazine,"* Vol. VII, No. 4, October, 1978. *"Coping with Conflict,"* by Judith Thurman, *"How to Avoid Conflict When You Can,"* by Kathryn Lee Girard, and *"How to Confront When You Have To"* by Kathryn Lee Girard. (370 Lexington Ave., N.Y., NY 10017, $1.50 for back issue.) Discusses women's socialization regarding conflict behavior, fear of conflict, and methods for coping with conflict.

Pfeiffer, J. William and John Jones, eds., *A HANDBOOK OF STRUCTURED EXPERIENCES FOR HUMAN RELATIONS TRAINING*, annual series, 1972 to present. University Associates Publishers, Inc. (7596 Eads Ave., La Jolla, CA 92037). A wide variety of exercises for use in groups and training situations. Activities range in diversity from problem-solving situations, to nonverbal communication, to male/female role plays. Most of the exercises are fairly complex or tightly structured. Thorough instructions are given.

Pfeiffer, J. William and John Jones, eds., *ANNUAL HANDBOOK FOR GROUP FACILITATORS*, 1972 to present. University Associates Publishers, Inc. (7596 Eads Ave., La Jolla, CA 92037). A wealth of how-to information coming out each year on how to work with groups. Include structured experiences, lecturettes, resources, research, theory, practice, and more.

*"Psychology Today,"* Vol. V, No. 6, November, 1971. *"Groupthink"* by Irving Janis, *"Selective Inattention"* by Ralph White, and *"Decisions, Decisions, Decisions"* by Jay Hall. Three articles concerned with group conformity in making decisions. The first two demonstrate how the conformity resulting from group dynamics at the top of hierarchies has led to disastrous decisions, including war. Hall's article defends group decision making's capacity for creativity. The series offers a view of what can happen when preconditions necessary for consensus are not met.

*"Quest: A Feminist Quarterly,"* Vol. IV, No. 4, Fall, 1978. *"The Process/Product Split"* by Ginny Crow, *"Integrating Process and Product"* by Dorothy Riddle, and *"Process/Product Split: A Misnomer"* by Caroline Sparks. (P.O. Box 8843, Washington, D.C., 20003.) These three articles discuss the "process/product debate" from three different perspectives. Addresses the problem: how do groups experience and value the tension between productive work and attention to process and human needs? The writers emphasize women's groups, but the issues raised are important to all.

**122**

Rice, Celeste, *"Face Saving, Criticism and Defensiveness,"* 1981. Center for Conflict Resolution (731 State St., Madison, WI 53703, $2). A well-researched article that integrates scholarly and experiential sources. Discusses the principles and skills for giving criticism in a way that can reduce defensiveness in both the sender and receiver of feedback.

Rosenberg, Marshall B. *FROM NOW ON: WITHOUT BLAME AND PUNISHMENT*, 1977. (Author's address: 3229 Bordeaux, Sherman, TX 75090, 214/893-3886, $3.50.) A personal approach to the skills of giving feedback and criticism in a way that promotes cooperation rather than conflict. Makes a persuasive statement about applying these techniques in all relationships.

Simon, Sidney B. *NEGATIVE CRITICISM . . . AND WHAT YOU CAN DO ABOUT IT*, 1978. Argus Communications. We disagree with this book's cleverly-depicted premise that criticism is almost always a bad thing. But it does make a number of good suggestions about how not to misuse criticism and offers good ideas about interpersonal validation.

Strongforce, Inc., *DEMOCRACY IN THE WORKPLACE: READINGS ON THE IMPLEMENTATION OF SELF MANAGEMENT IN AMERICA*, 1977. (2121 Decatur Place NW, Washington, D.C., $5.) A how-to for groups beginning a participatory business. Covers structural, organizational, legal and financial matters. A brief section on decision making.

Training/Action Affinity Group, *BUILDING SOCIAL CHANGE COMMUNITIES*, 1979. Movement for a New Society (4722 Baltimore Ave., Philadelphia, PA 19143, $2.80 + 70¢ postage.) Skills for creating and maintaining a collective or cooperative group, especially living communities. Excellent, concise chapters on consensus decision making, facilitation and conflict resolution.

Vocations for Social Change, *NO BOSSES HERE: A MANUAL ON WORKING COLLECTIVELY*, 1976. (353 Broadway, Cambridge, MA 02139, $3.) An overview of how to organize and operate a working collective. Includes discussions of decision making, meetings, common interpersonal problems as well as practical concerns such as finances and bookkeeping. Written in a personal, friendly style and draws on the experience of many collective members.

Walton, Richard, *INTERPERSONAL PEACE-MAKING: CONFRONTATIONS AND THIRD PARTY CONSULTATION*, 1969. Addison-Wesley Publishing Company. Provides a model for diagnosing recurring conflict between two parties and shows how a third-party facilitator can help interrupt and resolve the conflict. The theory is demonstrated with three in-depth case studies drawn from standard work situations.

Woodrow, Peter, *CLEARNESS: PROCESSES FOR SUPPORTING INDIVIDUALS AND GROUPS IN DECISION MAKING*, 1976. Movement for a New Society (4722 Baltimore Ave., Philadelphia, PA 19143, $1.75). This booklet describes a process groups can use to think through an issue carefully or to help a member do so. It is commonly used when deciding whether to accept a new member into a group and to help individuals make difficult personal decisions. *CLEARNESS* gives practical suggestions and sample agendas for having a clearness meeting.

Wyckoff, Hogie, ed., *LOVE, THERAPY AND POLITICS*, 1976. Grove Press, Inc., (196 W. Houston St., New York, NY 10014). This is a collection of articles compiled from the first year of *"Issues in Radical Therapy."* It includes political perspectives on therapy, group dynamics, male/female sex roles, and other concerns relevant to the practice of radical therapy.

Wyckoff, Hogie, *SOLVING WOMEN'S PROB-*
*LEMS (THROUGH AWARENESS, ACTION, AND*
*CONTACT)*, 1977. Grove Press, Inc.
(196 W. Houston St., New York, NY
10014). The lowdown on radical therapy principles and practice, positive
personal change that empowers individuals to work effectively for social
change. Describes the philosophy,
theory, and practical application of
problem-solving groups.

Yoast, Richard, *WHAT YOU CAN DO: A CITI-*
*ZEN'S GUIDE TO COMMUNITY ORGANIZING FOR*
*THE PREVENTION OF ALCOHOL, OTHER DRUG,*
*MENTAL HEALTH AND YOUTH PROBLEMS*, 1981.
The Wisconsin Clearinghouse (1954 E.
Washington, Madison, WI 53704). A work-
book for people organizing to work cooperatively for social change in a
community. Good information on leadership, group process, and especially on
defining goals and planning as a group.

"I do not go to a committee meeting merely to give my own ideas. If that were
all, I might write my fellow members a
letter. But neither do I go to learn
other people's ideas. If that were all,
I might ask each to write me a letter.
I go to a committee meeting in order that
all together we may create a group idea,
an idea which will be better than any of
our ideas alone, moreover which will be
better than all of our ideas added together. For this group idea will not be
produced by any process of addition, but
by the interpenetration of us all."

--Mary Parker Follett, *THE NEW STATE*
as quoted by INVERT

(Possible box to fit on page 92--contribution of new members.)

*a spectacular example in general!*
*—of reframing*
*—of value of "blocking"*

A living coop was trying to decide whether to ask a particular member, whose emotional disturbances were making life difficult for all, to move out of the house. Although the group normally operated by majority rule, they decided to strive for consensus since the issue was so sensitive. Most members felt that the situation had deteriorated to such a point that it was necessary to ask the problem member to leave. Everyone agreed except one person, the newest member of the group. She insisted that the group should try to pull together and give the problem member help and support. She came under considerable pressure from older group members who insisted that her newness meant that she didn't really know the full extent of the problem. Despite the pressure, however, the new member blocked consensus and did not permit the group to expell the problem member. Forced to make one last effort to work things out, the older members of the coop readjusted their viewpoints and found that they could sympathize with the problem member after all. The situation improved.

2000-3C3A002-82

Made in the USA
Columbia, SC
01 May 2020

95291554R00076